C0-AWE-521

SKETCHING A SCHEME

---

*A Friendship Model of Ministry
as a Mediating Structure*

Stuart Thomas Wilson

University Press of America,® Inc.
Lanham · Boulder · New York · Toronto · Oxford

Copyright © 2005 by
University Press of America,® Inc.
4501 Forbes Boulevard
Suite 200
Lanham, Maryland 20706
UPA Acquisitions Department (301) 459-3366

PO Box 317
Oxford
OX2 9RU, UK

All rights reserved
Printed in the United States of America
British Library Cataloging in Publication Information Available

Library of Congress Control Number: 2005924777
ISBN 0-7618-3222-X (clothbound : alk. ppr.)
ISBN 0-7618-3223-8 (paperback : alk. ppr.)

⊖™ The paper used in this publication meets the minimum
requirements of American National Standard for Information
Sciences—Permanence of Paper for Printed Library Materials,
ANSI Z39.48—1984

For Babbs

Contents

Acknowledgments

This book's basic text is that of my Columbia Theological Seminary Doctor of Ministry dissertation, minus two chapters and plus some minor changes. Therefore, I desire to give two directly related acknowledgements. Firstly, I want to express appreciation for the life and ministry of Columbia's now deceased professor emeritus of Systematic Theology, Dr. Shirley C. Guthrie, Jr. For thirty years I have benefited significantly from his work and witness. Secondly, I wish to thank all of the faculty, administration, staff and students of the Doctor of Ministry program with whom I interfaced. I am grateful to have been a part of such an engaging theological *milieu*.

Thirdly, I thankfully acknowledge that without the enduring encouragement and pastoral patience of my wife, Babbs, this book probably would not have been written.

Yet, these acknowledged persons are participants in a much larger group of life-assistants. Among many moving words of soliloquy, Alfred Tennyson (1974, Lines 18-21:88-89) in his poem "Ulysses" has the aged traveler utter an alluring observation:

I am a part of all that I have met;
Yet all experience is an arch wherethrough
Gleams that untravelled world, whose margin fades
For ever and for ever when I move.

I wish I could thank each archway-enabler by name and by specific commendation. That is not possible to do. Even if the production of a comprehensive roster were accomplished, it would only be the gathering of a small representative sample of the throng of persons who have helped me along the way of life and, thereby, also indirectly have helped me along the way of this book.

While a complete roll-call cannot be named, nevertheless, gratitude can be expressed for each and every member of that great cloud of witnesses. I continue to appreciate the ministering multitude of persons who have given countless gifts of challenge and comfort.

Introduction

There exists a provocative need for a model of ministry that functions as a mediating structure which mediates a Christian identity and a secular relevance. Many classical as well as modern models of ministry appear to stress either a Christian identity or a secular relevance. However, both qualities are essential to a comprehensive and current model of ministry.

An initial response to such a provocative need is the aim of this book: to submit the draft of a friendship model of ministry that stretches to be both traditionally faithful and worldly pertinent.

The primary dual issues of the project are how the church understands itself, Christian identity, and how the church understands its relationship to the world, secular relevance. The method of research will be an elementary investigation of sociology, theology and the pastorate in order to present the sketch of a friendship model of ministry as a sociological, a theological and a pastoral mediating structure, each of which mediates a Christian identity and a secular relevance.

The book makes the following progression. First, there is described the function of the friendship model of ministry as a mediating structure. Next, there is tendered the friendship model as a contemporary sociological mediating structure, as a normative theological mediating structure and as a prospective pastoral mediating structure. Lastly, there is conducted an examination of the friendship model of ministry in speculative reflection.

A further introduction is given by means of a general comparison, four qualifications and a specific voicing of that toward which the book moves.

In terms of a general comparison, the friendship model of ministry is a beginning attempt at being a sequel to the contemporary model of ministry as espoused by H. Richard Niebuhr in chapter two of his book, *The Purpose of the Church and Its Ministry* (1977:48-94). Niebuhr's chapter two is called, "The Emerging New Conception of the Ministry," and this title can be used to introduce the book's conception of ministry. However, Niebuhr's chapter title can be adopted as a comparative rubric only in the context of making several qualifications.

The first qualification is a list of disqualifications. On the whole and concerning its various portions, the book is impressionistic, incomplete, contrived and biased. The aptness of each one of these limitations will be ratified in due time. Therefore, all of these disaffirmations are seriously affirmed.

A second qualification is that the book operates, forthrightly and without lament, within the particular stream of 'postmodern' consciousness that presupposes all forms of legitimation are radically suspect. Deliberately then, the project is not a venture in legitimation. It is a venture in faith.

A third qualification is noted. Whenever the book is doing anything other than making a quotation, there are always three words that are always implicitly inferred even when they are not explicitly stated. It is categorically understood that, except for quotations, there is in front of every statement the following words: "in my opinion."

The fourth qualification is a cluster of meanings that the book projects into Niebuhr's title, "The Emerging New Conception of the Ministry." "Conception of the Ministry" supposes the conceptual framework of a model, which implies an abbreviated and a forced scheme. "Emerging" gratefully acknowledges the prior existence of the pieces to the model. "New" does not denote *creatio ex nihilo*. It means only the way in which the model's pieces are put together.

Finally, the proposed friendship model of ministry is also introduced by suggesting that it moves toward a clarification of a concept of identity and mission. May this draft contribute a tiny portion to that continuing, ambiguous alchemy of how the Church and humankind mix in the solution of history (Hodgson, 1989:11-50).[1]

Note

1. I am intentionally ambiguous in using the term "solution of history." "Solution" can be conceived of in terms of its chemical analogue and also in terms of being an answer to a problem. Both connotations are intended, but only in a provisional way. The solution of history is clearly not unambiguous. Furthermore, the solution of history may not be the classical answer of salvation history. For example, see Hodgson (1989:11-50) chapter 1, "Introduction: The End of Salvation History."

Chapter I

The Function of the Friendship Model of Ministry as a Mediating Structure

The function of the friendship model of ministry as a mediating structure is to be a friendship model of ministry as a mediating structure that mediates both a Christian identity and a secular relevance sociologically, theologically and pastorally, which is a ministerial model of Reformed spirituality. After briefly addressing several constituent parts of this functional statement, the chapter closes with a word of summary and a word of transition.

Is to be a Friendship Model

The function of the friendship model of ministry as a mediating structure is to be a friendship model. What is first underlined here is the noun "model." As stated in the "Introduction," the conceptual framework of a model "implies an abbreviated and a forced scheme." All models, then, have an innate weakness and a limited strength. What is next alluded to is the adjective "friendship." While commentary on and expansion of the friendship model happen later in the book, now the model is presented only in its barest form.

A Friendship Model of Ministry

Label:	Friend
Task:	Witness to Jesus Christ, the revelation of God's friendship of suffering and liberating love with humankind
Object:	Freedom of God's friendship with humankind
Place:	Church, home, community, world
Whom served:	God and humankind

Is to be a Friendship Model of Ministry

The function of the friendship model of ministry as a mediating structure is to be a friendship model of ministry. The friendship model of ministry is not a technique of control that is used to manipulate the ministry or persons. It is not a technique of measurement that is used to identify degrees of so-called faithfulness. There is always an indefinable, mysterious element in life that lives, however imperfectly, in the knowledge and presence of the living God (The Vocation Agency:6).[1] Hence, the proposed friendship model is neither an instrument of arrogance that assumes one can justify one's ministry, nor is the model an instrument of insecurity that assumes one must justify one's ministry. Rather, the operative understanding is that ministry is both a gift and a task from God, in which there is a receiving and a giving in response to divine grace. Therefore, the model is an attempt at being disciplined and responsible in following the calling of ministry. Consequently, the model's efficacy depends on the work of the Holy Spirit and on disciplined human work in response to grace.

Is to be a Friendship Model of Ministry as a Mediating Structure

The function of the friendship model of ministry as a mediating structure is to be a friendship model of ministry as a mediating structure.

Peter Berger in the book *Facing Up to Modernity* promulgates the concept of an institutional mediating structure.

> What are mediating structures? The concept has vast implications, but it can be defined simply: mediating structures are those institutions which stand between the individual in his [and her] private sphere and the large institutions of the public sphere. . . . These are, precisely, the mediating institutions . . . of family, church, voluntary association, neighborhood, and subculture. (1977:132,134)[2]

While the concept of mediating structures is not new, the disintegration of contemporary mediating structures that is due to modernization is new.

> Modernization brings about a novel dichotomization of social life. The dichotomy is between the huge and immensely powerful institutions of the public sphere (the state, the large economic agglomerates that we now know as corporations and labor unions, and the ever-growing bureaucracies that administer sectors of society not properly political or economic, such as education or the organized professions) and the private sphere, which is a curious interstitial area "left over," as it were, by the large institutions . . . Put more simply, the dichotomy is between the megastructures and private life. (Berger, 1977:133)

The weakening of contemporary mediating structures due to modernization manufactures a double dilemma.

> The progressive disintegration of mediating structures constitutes a double crisis, on the level of individual life and also on a political level. Without mediating structures, private life comes to be engulfed in a deepening anomie. Without mediating structures, the political order is drawn into the same anomie by being deprived of the moral foundation upon which it rests. (Berger, 1977:135)

A rearticulation of and application of the concept of mediating structures is not an absolute antidote for internal and external *anomie*. It may be a fruitful place to begin to discover some new possibilities.

However, the friendship model of ministry is obviously not an institutional mediating structure. The model is not an institution: it is a conceptual mediating structure. Furthermore, the model is not a conceptual mediating structure that originates from the dynamics of mega-public life and the model is not a conceptual mediating structure that originates from the dynamics of individual-private life. The friendship model of ministry is, instead, conceived of as a conceptual mediating structure of the church as an institutional mediating structure.

Is to be a Friendship Model of Ministry as a Mediating Structure that Mediates

The function of the friendship model of ministry as a mediating structure is to be a friendship model of ministry as a mediating structure that mediates. The meaning of the verb "to mediate," as used in the context of the model which mediates, is not the meaning of "to arbitrate" or "to synthesize." The meaning is "to give expression." However, the meaning is not to give expression in an uncoordinated fashion. Rather, the intended sense is "to give material expression" according to a formal principle. The formal principle is not a principle that is contained in or can be derived from the friendship model of ministry. The formal principle can be interpreted as being the friendship model itself and, therefore, the friendship model itself in its intension and extension is the formal principle. The intended meaning of "to mediate," then, is "to give material expression according to the model as a formal principle."

Is to be a Friendship Model of Ministry as a Mediating Structure that Mediates both a Christian Identity and a Secular Relevance

The function of a friendship model of ministry as a mediating structure is to be a friendship model of ministry as a mediating structure that mediates both a Christian identity and a secular relevance. By "Christian identity" what is implied is not a Christian identity that is parochial, but a basic Christian identity which can be considered to be ecumenical.[3] However, this basic Christian identity is not so distinctive that it has no secular relevance. Rather, the model's Christian identity issues forth in a secular relevance. On the other hand, the model's secular relevance does not become so relevant in a secular way that it loses its distinctive Christian identity. Christian identity and secular relevance exist in a symbiotic relationship. A crisis in one produces a crisis in the other. Jurgen Moltmann in *The Crucified God* says that

> . . . the crisis of relevance and the crisis of identity are complementary to each other. Where identity is found, relevance is called into question. Where relevance is achieved, identity is called into question. We can now define this double crisis more closely with regard to Christian faith, by saying that each of these crises is simply a reflection of the other. . . .(1974:25)

Such a crisis of and between a Christian identity and a secular relevance is an intrinsic and an inevitable crisis. The crisis is necessarily endemic and pandemic of Christian faith and practice.

This necessary tension of Christian faith and practice is further depicted by Moltmann when he writes in *Theology Today* about Christian theology as being a "mediating theology":

> In historical terms, any Christian theology is a "mediating theology" whether or not it is aware of the fact, since it mediates the Christian message that has been handed down in such a way that it falls within the horizons of the understanding of the people of a particular time. Mediation between the Christian tradition and the culture of the present is the most important task of theology. Without a living relationship to the possibilities and problems of the man or woman of the present, Christian theology becomes sterile and irrelevant. But without reference to the Christian tradition Christian theology becomes opportunist and uncritical. Historical mediation must both work to achieve the true preservation of the identity of the Christian message and see that it is relevant to the present. Christian theology has succeeded in making great syntheses in its history. For centuries the theology of the early church was a successful and well-tried synthesis between Christian tradition and Hellenistic culture. While the Reformation again concentrated entirely on the identity of the biblical Christian proclamation, it became effective in culture only as a result of the Protestant humanism of Melanchthon and Calvin, which has shaped the modern world in Western and Central Europe. However, so far Christian theology has not yet succeeded in arriving at a single, generally convincing, synthesis in the perspective of modern culture. The phenomenon of "modernity" is too unclear and too varied. The modern spirit questions each tradition and especially each religious tradition too critically, and relativizes it. So in the face of the specific problems of this modern world the mediating theology of the Christian tradition has a twofold

task. On the one hand it must defend the right and the significance of
Christian faith against the doubt and the criticism of the modern spirit
apologetically. On the other hand it must show that the Christian faith
has therapeutic relevance to the sicknesses of the modern spirit and the
perplexities of the modern world. The present-day mediation of Christian faith to the modern world is always determined by apologetic
interests on the one hand and by interests which are critical of culture
and therapeutic on the other. That distinguishes modern "mediating
theology" from its predecessors in the pre-modern eras. (1989:53-54)

Moltmann continues his treatment by casting the contextual charac-
ters which challenge today's mediating theology. The provocative challenge is to try to negotiate a creative dialogue out of four divergent major
works toward mediation in the modern world:

1. Existential theology: Rudolf Bultmann and the problem of
    history.
2. Transcendental theology: Karl Rahner and the problem of
    anthropocentricity.
3. Cultural theology: Paul Tillich and the religious interpreta-
    tion of the secular world.
4. Political theology and imperfect modernity. (1989:57-94)

It is ridiculous even to speculate that any model can function adequately as a sole mediating structure for the inclusion of and the critique
of these four diverse perspectives. However, not to attempt at any level
to participate in a mediating conversation is not to be engaged in serious,
contemporary, theological discussion. The function of the friendship model
of ministry as a mediating structure speaks only minimally and vaguely
in the direction of this potential mediating dialogue.

Is to be a Friendship Model of Ministry as a Mediating Structure that Mediates both a Christian Identity and a Secular Relevance Sociologically, Theologically and Pastorally

The function of the friendship model of ministry as a mediating structure
is to be a friendship model of ministry as a mediating structure that

mediates both a Christian identity and a secular relevance sociologically, theologically and pastorally. In short, the friendship model of ministry is one way of attempting to mediate both a Christian identity and a secular relevance sociologically, theologically and pastorally. The model's methodology begins to explore a small portion of sociology, theology and the pastorate for a purpose that can be framed in two ways.

First, the subjects can be "Christian identity" and "secular relevance." The method of research proceeds by mediating a Christian identity and a secular relevance by means of a sociological mediating structure, a theological mediating structure and a pastoral mediating structure. The second way of framing the model's movement of discourse is for the subject to be "a mediating structure." Sentenced in this way, the method of research views three forms of a mediating structure: a sociological mediating structure that has a Christian identity and a secular relevance, a theological mediating structure that has a Christian identity and a secular relevance and a pastoral mediating structure that has a Christian identity and a secular relevance. Regardless of whether the subject is posed as being either "Christian identity-secular relevance" or "a mediating structure," the operation of the model organizes for the purpose of fulfilling in substance the same superintending function, which is to express variously both a Christian identity and a secular relevance.

As previously implied, it is understood that the qualities of a Christian identity and a secular relevance are non-negotiable. The model's Christian identity—which is "witness to Christ"—is constantly present, whether it is found in a sociological mediating structure and/or a theological mediating structure and/or a pastoral mediating structure. The model's secular relevance—which is "God and humankind being served in church, home, community and world by a witness to Christ"—remains intact as it is described sociologically and/or theologically and/or pastorally. It is hoped that the book's methodology will manifest a friendship model of ministry that expresses at least some sociological, theological and pastoral validity in its circuitous quest out of and for identity and relevance.

Is to be a Friendship Model of Ministry as a Mediating Structure that Mediates both a Christian Identity and a Secular Relevance Sociologically, Theologically and Pastorally, Which is a Ministerial Model of Reformed Spirituality

The function of the friendship model of ministry as a mediating structure is to be a friendship model of ministry as a mediating structure that mediates both a Christian identity and a secular relevance sociologically, theologically and pastorally, which is a ministerial model of Reformed spirituality.

Often ministry seems unspiritual and spirituality seems non-ministerial. However, maybe a Reformed view of both ministry and spirituality can attempt to put the two together formally and materially.[4] The result of such a union would mean that a spiritual model of Reformed ministry is equivalent to a ministerial model of Reformed spirituality.

Spirituality can be thought of as being a cognitive, affective and behavioral open-life system of a universal theological world view. The adjective "Reformed" locates the tradition from which and by which ministry and spirituality will be qualified. In his *Growing in the Life of Christian Faith*, Craig Dystra gives an excellent, brief description of the "Reformed tradition."

> The phrase "the Reformed tradition" is widely used to refer to a particular church historical movement that began in the 16th century in Western Europe and is still alive today in churches and to patterns of life and thought that have emerged in historical continuity with those beginnings. The tradition is marked by certain central theological themes and convictions as well as by key theologians and writings (including creeds and confessions) through which these themes and convictions have been articulated in various circumstances over the centuries. The tradition is also marked by certain practices: patterns of liturgy, governance, personal and corporate discipline, and service. . . . [One may] frequently speak of what the Reformed tradition holds, believes, thinks, or says. There is some danger in doing this, so several cautions are in order. First, the tradition is not static. Its central themes and convictions and practices have undergone modification (sometimes sig-

nificant) over time. Therefore, we cannot simply pluck statements out of any particular document and be sure that a whole movement is thereby represented. Second, the tradition has always been to some degree pluralistic. At no point in time has there been agreement on everything by everyone. Thus, the tradition itself is as much an ongoing argument as it is a relative consensus. Third, a tradition is not the sort of thing to have clear boundaries, and discerning what may be said to be "Reformed" is often a matter of context and perspective. No single reading of the tradition, therefore, has a purchase on defining it. Fourth, the Reformed tradition both influences and is influenced by the many cultures and contexts in which it has lived over time. The result is that its practices and beliefs have naturally become more inclusive and pluralistic than those of its formative years. Finally, most of what the Reformed tradition holds, it holds in common with all other Christian churches and people. Thus, when we speak of what the Reformed tradition holds, believes, or does, we are not necessarily— or even usually—talking about what the Reformed tradition holds exclusively, distinctively, or apart from others. Indeed, one of the fundamental characteristics of the Reformed tradition is its ecumenical commitment, its openness to other Christians and to all persons.

The phrase "the Reformed tradition" is, therefore, a kind of shorthand. And while it admittedly may oversimplify (and thereby somewhat distort) the complexity of the actual historical situation, it is nonetheless a useful term for calling to mind a stream of life and thought that has identifiable contours in reality. Sometimes such a stream may seem so forceful and overwhelming that one fears drowning in it. But it may also be a current that lifts one up, carries one along, and provides direction as well as refreshment. (37)

A Reformed tradition is fully acknowledged as part of the book's bias in dealing with a concept of ministerial spirituality. Nevertheless, such a bias is not immune to critical analysis. Hence, there will be a drawing from a limited investigation of sociology, theology and the pastorate in order to be able to conduct a beginning discussion toward the formation of a ministerial model of reformed spirituality.

The guiding spiritual principle of the friendship model of ministry is that ministry equals life as a calling from God. The guiding spiritual principle of life as a calling from God is prayer.[5] A life of prayer receives the necessary grace of wisdom and strength which continually informs, adjudicates, and coordinates the entire personal and professional life of Reformed spirituality (Barth, 1991:92). Prayer is the paradigm of the spiritual life (Barth, 1991:44). Prayer is not only ". . . the chief exercise of faith . . . by which we daily receive God's benefits" (Calvin:850), prayer, as well as ministry, is also ". . . both a gift and a task from God, in which there is a receiving and a giving in response to divine grace."[6] Likewise, the spiritual life is "both a gift and a task from God, in which there is a receiving and a giving in response to divine grace." Thus, prayer is the paradigm of the Christian spiritual life, ministerial and otherwise (Barth, 1991:43-44).

In addition to the hope for ministry and spirituality to be connected, there is also the hope for a ministerial model of Reformed spirituality that possesses and can mediate the two previously proposed non-negotiable characteristics: a Christian identity and a secular relevance. Many classical as well as modern models of ministry and of spirituality seem to emphasize either a Christian identity or a secular relevance. Yet, both qualities are essential to an adequate, comprehensive, contemporary ministerial model of Reformed spirituality. Concomitantly, a Christian identity and a secular relevance give a ministerial model a Reformed spiritual character. This spiritual character seeks to hallow the whole of life. To hallow the whole of life by a holistic witness to Christ is both the function of and the goal of a spiritual model of Reformed ministry, which is tantamount to being a ministerial model of Reformed spirituality.

A Word of Summary and a Word of Transition

It is recognized that all human relationships, including those within a Reformed spiritual community, can involve a good sense of creatureliness, always involve a sinful sense of creatureliness and may involve the inspiring presence of God (Alston:71-93). Therefore, because of this recognition and because the function of the friendship model of ministry is to mediate sociologically, theologically and pastorally a Christian identity and a secular relevance, the proposed model is not purely idealistic. It welcomes reality.

Yet, in view of the function of the friendship model of ministry as a mediating structure, the model may appear to be simplistic. It may also appear to have the potential for expansion. Subsequent writing will present the friendship model as a contemporary sociological mediating structure, as a normative theological mediating structure and as a prospective pastoral mediating structure, each of which aims to mediate both a Christian identity and a secular relevance. These presentations are far from being plenary. Nevertheless, despite its fragmentary expressions, the friendship model of ministry is offered for serious examination.

Notes

1. The Vocation Agency (6) expresses this idea in its introduction:

. . .[T]he quality of spiritual life in a particular minister is beyond measurement and may be the most important factor in the minister's impact upon a congregation and the world around it. There is an element of mystery in ministry, and the Holy Spirit does not always act through persons in predictable ways. However, it is possible to determine the roles that must be fulfilled if the mission of the church is to be carried forward. The specific actions involved may be described in such a way that levels of performance are established and may be used in assessing the work of an individual.

2. See Berger (1977:130-141) chapter 11, "In Praise of Particularity: The Concept of Mediating Structures."

3. The friendship model of ministry may be construed, by some whim of the imagination, to have some significance for various portions of the Church universal. However, the book's focus is with Reformed families of faith.

4. See Barth (1981:79) concerning any attempt to organize spirituality, even in a ministerial fashion. It is instructive to remember a descriptive paragraph of Barth which ends with an arresting axiom about spiritual life:

From this standpoint, the art of liturgical worship, ordered and shaped by historical models and aesthetic ideals, although it has again come to be highly rated today, is an enterprise that is by no means free from suspicion. The same applies to a systematically constructed theory and practice of individual spiritual formation along the lines of the *Exercises* of Ignatius as these are still followed today both in and beyond Roman Catholic circles. The good that there might be in such attempts— and who is so bold as to rule out at once the possibility of good?—can perhaps be claimed as good from the Christian standpoint only in spite of their character as techniques, not because of it. Perspicacious friends of Christian liturgy and mysticism (including the so-called "little"

Theresa of Lisieux) have not usually concealed this either from themselves or others. Spiritual life . . . begins at the very point where spiritual skill ends.

5. For a refreshing discussion of prayer, see Barth (1960b:265-288, 1961a:87-115). A rich and challenging articulation of prayer as the impression and expression of the Lord's Prayer is also found in Barth (1981:47-271).

6. This idea is first mentioned in chapter 1, under the section "Is to Be a Friendship Model of Ministry," page 2.

Chapter II

The Friendship Model of Ministry as a Contemporary Sociological Mediating Structure

This chapter first looks at the friendship model of ministry as a contemporary sociological mediating structure in relationship to community, friendship and self-interest, and then in relationship to modernity, Niebuhr's analysis, ministerial functions, communal disciplined practices, faith and to society.

In Relationship to Community, Friendship and Self-Interest

The friendship model of ministry as a contemporary sociological mediating structure is not a proponent of the church as an intimacy group. It does not prescribe an exclusive and segmental lifestyle enclave: it prescribes an inclusive and integrated community. Bellah and his associates in *Habits of the Heart* searingly discern these contrasting characteristics.

> . . . Whereas a community attempts to be an inclusive whole, celebrating the interdependence of public and private life and of the different callings of all, lifestyle is fundamentally segmental and celebrates the narcissism of similarity. It usually explicitly involves a contrast with others who "do not share one's lifestyle." For this reason, we speak not of lifestyle communities, though they are often called such in contemporary usage, but of lifestyle enclaves. Such enclaves are segmen-

tal in two senses. They involve only a segment of each individual, for
they concern only private life, especially leisure and consumption.
And they are segmental socially in that they include only those with a
common lifestyle. (72)

Rather than having a constituency of individuals who are personally and
socially fragmented, the friendship model of ministry as a contemporary
sociological mediating structure organizes in order to build, nurture and
guide a community that is comprised of people who are personally and
socially integrated.

The friendship model of ministry also advocates a sociological description of friendship. Again conferring with Bellah and his friends in
Habits of the Heart, the principle of classical friendship is introduced.

The conception of friendship put forward by Aristotle, elaborated by
Cicero, and understood for centuries in the context of the Christian
conception of personhood, was well known to Americans in colonial
and early republican times. Since contemporary ideas of friendship are
heavily influenced by the therapeutic attitude, it is worth remembering
that the traditional idea of friendship had three essential components.
Friends must enjoy one another's company, they must be useful to one
another, and they must share a common commitment to the good.
(115)

Another quality that may be implied in these three components needs to
be made explicit. To the classical ingredients of the concept of friendship, a fourth factor can be included: that of respect (Moltmann,
1977:316).[1] All four elements mutually support and encourage one another.

Later, the same authors illuminate Tocqueville's "vision of the public good founded on enlightened self-interest" (174). What is endorsed
here is not the brand of community, friendship and self-interest that is
expounded by our current North American culture. On the contrary, the
model suggests that these three components—inclusive community,
ammended classical friendship and enlightened self-interest—combine
and transform each other and be directed toward the ecclesiastical, fa-
miliar, communal and global good. This formative conscious and unconscious process can exert a formidable ethical power for the public good.[2]

In Relationship to Modernity[3]

The ensuing travelogue traces the friendship model's spiritual pilgrimage and, thereby, tracks the model's desire to minister across a contemporary sociological, theological and pastoral terrain.

As a first step, the friendship model of ministry attempts to transcend the futurity of the modern world, which predicts the future as being qualitatively better than past and present time. A Christian interpretation of history, in which this model is activated, announces the faith statement that the past, the present and the future are all significant, singularly and collectively. Also, the future is not inherently progressive: it is ambiguously and simultaneously infused with crisis and infused with hope. Christ, who is the revelation of the meaning of history (Berkhof, 1962), is the divine sign of both crisis and of hope (Moltmann, 1977:47-50).

The model attempts to transcend the secularization of the modern world by proclaiming the active, mysterious presence of the living God in a good yet fallen world that is created, sustained, governed, judged, reconciled and redeemed by God. Thus, despite the absurdity of evil and the sickness of sin, the universe has meaning and, therefore, our ethical participation in the world has meaning.

The friendship model of ministry attempts to transcend the individualism of the modern world. The matrix of individualism (the bifurcation of church-state, private-public, value-fact, belief-knowing, feeling-knowledge, personal-impersonal, intimacy group-megastructure) is unified by the bridge of a public community of friends. Neither a public megastructure nor a lifestyle enclave, a public community of friends is a sociological subculture that has its own unique mediating structure. The following list mentions briefly the general characteristics of a public community as a sociological mediating structure: (a) is not small; (b) is diverse in make-up and beliefs; (c) is composed of friendly strangers who do human things, but are not intimate friends; (d) has a voluntary organizational structure that encourages participation, yet is not a pure democracy; (e) has public beliefs and goals that allow for dissent and doubt; (f) is a part of a larger organization that requires some compliance; (g) has professional leadership which stands, in some respects, outside the structure; and (h) is publicly under the judgment and grace of God.[4]

Because of its voluntary configuration, a public community of friends is actualized by a leader who can be likened unto a particular kind of politician. In his book, *The Church*, Wallace Alston gives four basic representations of "The Minister as Politician."

> First, the minister, like the politician, is accountable to a constitu-ency. . . . Second, to say that the ministerial task is a political task is to say that the minister must be an effective communicator or teacher. . . . Third, the minister as a politician must have a sense of vocation that transcends mere professionalism and gives to the ministry the identity of a sacred calling. . . . Finally, the ministry requires considerable courage. There are times when the minister, like the politician, runs into trouble. There are times when the minister fails to develop a Chris-tian consensus with the constituency, when conscience calls the minis-ter to stand over against the membership of the church, and when the minister must run the risk of losing a grip on the job. (117-119)

Such a "minister as politician" must build, nurture and guide the public community of friends into realizing its unique opportunities: (1) to live with benevolent strangers without fear and in cooperation on com-mon life in order to learn civility; (2) to let persons be themselves with support; (3) to challenge affirmatively growth in faith; (4) to tolerate and encourage diversity and conflict with survival; (5) to provide the oppor-tunity for worship of God and celebration; (6) to provide the opportunity of intimacy groups without their becoming ultimate; (7) to be a part of a friendly and benign structure; (8) to discover and to affirm one's voca-tion and ministry in the church and the world; (9) to cultivate communal memory and hope; and (10) to articulate an alternative value system.[5]

The public community of a church congregation is a constituted com-munity of mediating friendships where there is communal meaning, be-longing, memory, structure, values, caring and mission. Thus, the friend-ship model as a contemporary sociological mediating structure speaks to the basic needs of our individualistic North American society. Bellah and his co-authors depict nine needs of our society's individualism. It may be instructive to do a quick viewing of the following dynamics in order to see how these nine sociological needs might begin to be met by and in a ministerial model of the church as a public community of friends. (1) Instead of or in spite of leaving home, one is welcomed into a new ex-tended family of friends. (2) Instead of having a blank slate upon which to write one's own religious choice, the nurturing community of friends can offer background information and experience as a spring-board to the spiritual quest. (3) Instead of the work of a career, an intrinsically valuable vocational call can be discovered in the community of friends. (4) Instead of self-authentication through the prioritizing of values based upon personal preference, the company of friends articulates an enduring community value system based on a communal constitution. (5) Instead of the lifestyle enclave form of 'community' for individuals, the constituted fellowship of friends is a public community. (6) Instead of the fragile and frantic narcissism of the therapeutic concept of love and marriage, a public community of friends enables the adventure of lasting commitments of love and marriage where self is not the only center. (7) Instead of a lifestyle enclave, the church is a public community of friends that exists for the communal and societal good. (8) Instead of involvement in public life, and (9) instead of involvement in national policy for the purpose of following personal agendas, the community of friends participates in society in a way that is similar to its communal participation: it has inherent value directed toward the public good.[6]

The fortified concept and model of friendship not only bridges the private-public matrix of individuated life, it preaches the interrelationship of individual concern, communal concern, societal concern and ultimate concern. In the fellowship of this public community of friends, enduring commitments can be made to God, family, love and marriage, community and society. Here there can be found an intrinsically meaningful and rewarding calling in life, a calling that can also help to transform society with civil and personal friendships and humane, friendly structures. Self, other persons, world and God start to coalesce within the social, economic and political process, making available a creative sense of personal fulfillment, societal integration and cosmic relatedness.

The ministerial model of friendship also attempts to transcend the pluralism of the modern world. Aimless pluralism may be transcended by the formation within the public community of friends of a general consensus about what constitutes life and, therefore, by the formation of a community of meaning, value and direction. Within this general constitutional structure, there exists a high degree of freedom that allows the free expression of a rich diversity of thought, value and action.

Modern pluralism and individualism in the church may be transcended by the friendship model of ministry which goes beyond orthodoxy, pietism and liberalism (Guthrie, 1986). The overall thrust of the model is theocentric and not egocentric. Persons are not called to advertise themselves and their individualistic and pluralistic thoughts, feelings, actions, or even friendships. They are summoned to participate in the primary and unifying task of being witnesses to Jesus Christ.

Such a witness to God's presence in the world transfigures the church's and culture's popular individualistic and pluralistic notions of success, freedom and justice. Bellah and company want to keep alive the biblical, republican, utilitarian and expressive strands of our contemporary North American culture. With the intrinsic potential of these four ethnological strands, they also want to transform the popular concepts of success, freedom and justice. Success is not ". . . material wealth, but the creation of a community in which a genuinely ethical and spiritual life . . . can be lived"(29). True freedom is participation in this kind of community. Justice is the working toward a more inclusive participation of the free expression of this community.

Thus, the friendship model of ministry as a contemporary sociological mediating structure may be able to begin to minister to the current North American society and church which is influenced by modernity, as it attempts to transcend futurity, secularism, individualism and pluralism. In so doing, it creates an alternative communal context and experience of meaning, value and direction. However, Craig Dykstra delivers an insightful message in *Growing in the Life of Christian Faith*:

> We affirm that Christian faith begins with God, with God's presence with and love for the world, rather than with what we want for ourselves. Thus, the meaning and point of Christian faith is not simply (or, even primarily) to meet human yearnings for meaning, value, and direction. Nonetheless, we confess and give thanks that in the life of Christian faith meaning, value, and direction are provided in such richness and depth that our hungers for them, while often transformed, are indeed met. (3)

In the proposed friendship model of ministry, ontological individualism and empty individualism are abolished. Utilitarian individualism and expressive individualism are transformed.[7]

In Relationship to Niebuhr's Analysis

Next, is a gleaning from some different models of ministry that have appeared throughout history, as revealed by H. Richard Niebuhr's book *The Purpose of the Church and Its Ministry* (1977:48-94).[8] Niebuhr demonstrates that a model of ministry is an image which shapes the whole of ministry, granting it order, consistency and prioritization.

> . . . Since the days described in the New Testament Christian ministers have preached and taught; they have led worship and administered sacraments; they have presided over the church and exercised oversight over its work; they have given pastoral care to individuals in need. Though at times these functions have been distributed among specialized orders of the clergy, still each minister, in his [and her] own domain, has needed to exercise all of them. Yet whenever there has been a clear conception of the office one of these functions has been regarded as central and the other functions have been ordered so as to serve, not indeed it, but, the chief purpose that it served directly. (1977:58-59)

The theme of coordination is further accentuated through the parameters in which and by which a model of ministry attains unity. This is the unity of a formal and material simplicity.

> As these [following] examples of typical ideas of the ministry all indicate, a clear-cut conception always includes not only an understanding of what the most important work of the ministry is, but also the recognition that it must perform other functions. Unity is given to such a conception not only by ordering functions in a scale of importance but by directing each function to a chief, though still proximate, end. (1977:62-63)

A chart[9] is now presented of Niebuhr's sociological, theological and pastoral analysis of the various models of ministry[10] that have been underscored throughout a portion of the Church's history.[11]

An Historical Chart of Ministerial Models

adapted from H. Richard Niebuhr's book, *The Purpose of the Church and Its Ministry* in Chapter Two, "The Emerging New Conception of the Ministry"

Historical Period	Purpose and Work		Call "Focus"	Authority "Focus"	Whom Served
Middle Ages	Label:	Pastoral Ruler	Ecclesiastical	Personal discipline	Church
	Task:	Government of Souls			
	Object:	Salvation in life to come			
	Place:	Cathedral			
Reformation	Label:	Teacher/Preacher	Providential	Scripture	Church
	Task:	Declare God's love and forgiveness			
	Object:	Renewal of life via evangelical faith			
	Place:	Pulpit/Auditorium			
Wesleyan	Label:	Evangelist	Secret	Personal Experience	World
	Task:	Persuasive preaching			
	Object:	Conversion			
	Place:	Outside the church, tent, brush arbor			
Catholic	Label:	Priest/Minister	Ecclesiastical	Institutional	Church
	Task:	Eucharistic mediation			
	Object:	Reconciliation			
	Place:	Altar			
Contemporary	Label:	Pastoral Director	Christian, Providential	Communal	Church
	Task:	"Building up"			
	Object:	That the church may do its ministry			
	Place:	Office			

For a helpful discussion on the concept of the authority focus, see Niebuhr's section "The Minister's Authority" (1977:66-74). Concerning the call focus, Niebuhr first italicizes and then amplifies a vocal quartet:

It appears that there is general though only implicit recognition of the fact that a call to the ministry includes at least these four elements: (1) the *call to be a Christian,* which is variously described as the call to discipleship of Jesus Christ, to hearing and doing of the Word of God, to repentance and faith, et cetera; (2) *the secret call,* namely, that inner persuasion or experience whereby a person feels . . . directly summoned or invited by God to take up the work of the ministry; (3) *the providential call,* which is that invitation and command to assume the work of the ministry which comes through the equipment of a person with the talents necessary for the exercise of the office and through the divine guidance of . . . [one's] life by all its circumstances; (4) *the ecclesiastical call,* that is, the summons and invitation extended to a . . . [person] by some community or institution of the Church to engage in the work of the ministry. (1977:64)

Included in and beyond a call to ministry is a call for salvation. Niebuhr's analysis gives credence to a provoking reality: the symphonic cry for salvation is historically interpreted and orchestrated by each generation and performed by each epoch. In directing the modern cry for salvation, Niebuhr joins Paul Tillich in synthesizing the ultimate moaning . . .

. . . in terms of disruption, conflict, self-destruction, meaninglessness, and despair in all realms of life. . . . The question arising out of this experience is not, as in the Reformation, the question of a merciful God and the forgiveness of sins; nor is it, as in the early Greek church, the question of infinitude, of death and error; nor is it the question of the personal religious life, or of the Christianization of culture and society. It is the question of a reality of reconciliation and reunion, of creativity, meaning and hope. (177:93)

Niebuhr asserts that this is, indeed, a cry for salvation and rebirth. It is a puzzle then why it is that Niebuhr, in the construction of the contemporary model of ministry, does not describe the person who gives the answer to this cry as some kind of prophet, as one may have expected. Instead, according to Niebuhr, the sagest respondent happens to be a pastoral director, who works out of an office and who has the task of "building up so that the church may do its ministry." The form of the theological answer does not seem to harmonize with the form of the existential question.

The similarity between the proposed friendship model of ministry and Niebuhr's contemporary model is that in both there is a "building up so that the Church may do its ministry." There are several dissimilarities. The tasks and the objects are different. In the proposed model, both the church and the world are served, while the authority focus consists of all five, that is, institutional, communal, scripture, personal discipline and personal experience. The call focus is inclusive: Christian, ecclesiastical, providential and secret. Also, all of the labels, tasks, objects and places of each of the historical models can find some activity at some time in the operation of the proposed ministerial construct, which is once again presented in bare form.

A Friendship Model of Ministry

Label (Identity):	Friend
Task (Purpose):	Witness to Jesus Christ, the revelation of God's friendship of suffering and liberating love with humankind
Object (Aim):	Freedom of God's friendship with humankind
Place:	Church, home, community, world
Whom Served:	God and humankind

The terms "label," "task," "object," "place" and "whom served" are taken from Niebuhr's historical chart. The terms "identity," "purpose" and "aim" are additions that are given in the hope of clarification and augmentation.

The use of the concept of "identity" may need some explanation. First of all, each one of the functions of ministry that soon will be described is exercised by a person who is both a friend and a witness: a friend who is a witness and a witness who is a friend. Therefore, the label (identity) could be titled "witnessing friend."

Moreover, the depth of ministry is not authenticated by merely assuming certain ministerial roles and acting out divergent functions. A ministry that is sound in substance and principle actualizes its potential as it discovers a singular, profound, integral identity which can be expressed variously through myriad functions. Consequently, all of the functions are integrated with each other and, in turn, all are integrated with the originating, essential identity. There is a potential merger here with functional integration and personal integration. This core merger confers upon the friendship model of ministry the possibility of a meaningful and powerful integrity.

In Relationship to Ministerial Functions

The seven functional agents of the friendship model of ministry are preacher-worship leader, visitor-counselor, teacher, missionary, administrator, judicatory member (member of judicatories) and professional member (member of the profession of ministry). In each of these functions, the label (identity) of the minister is that of a friend:

- a preacher-worship leader friend who facilitates worship;
- a visitor-counselor friend who facilitates pastoral care;
- a teacher friend who facilitates Christian education;
- a missionary friend who facilitates mission;
- an administrator friend who facilitates administration;
- a judicatory friend who facilitates judicatory activities;
- a professional friend who facilitates professional development.

Each function is exercised in a community of worshipping, caring, teaching-learning, missionary, administrative, judicatory and professional friends. Furthermore, although there are seven different functional expressions of friend, the task (purpose) of each function is the same: to witness to Jesus Christ, the revelation of God's friendship of suffering and liberating love with humankind. The object (aim) is also identical: the freedom, or increase, of God's friendship with humankind.

Although the following elucidation is obviously apparent, for the sake of completeness a summary is offered in redundant detail as to how the friendship model of ministry coordinates its seven-fold functioning:

- a preacher-worship leader friend who witnesses to Jesus Christ, the revelation of God's friendship of suffering and liberating love with humankind, with a community of worshipping friends whose object (aim) is the increasing freedom of God's friendship with humankind;

- a visitor-counselor friend who witnesses to Jesus Christ, the revelation of God's friendship of suffering and liberating love with humankind, with a community of caring friends whose object (aim) is the increasing freedom of God's friendship with humankind;

- a teacher friend who witnesses to Jesus Christ, the revelation of God's friendship of suffering and liberating love with humankind, with a community of teaching-learning friends whose object (aim) is the increasing freedom of God's friendship with humankind;

- a missionary friend who witnesses to Jesus Christ, the revelation of God's friendship of suffering and liberating love with humankind, with a community of missionary friends whose object (aim) is the increasing freedom of God's friendship with humankind;

- an administrator friend who witnesses to Jesus Christ, the revelation of God's friendship of suffering and liberating love with humankind, with a community of administrative friends whose object (aim) is the increasing freedom of God's friendship with humankind;

- a judicatory friend who witnesses to Jesus Christ, the revelation of God's friendship of suffering and liberating love with humankind, with a community of judicatory friends whose object (aim) is the increasing freedom of God's friendship with humankind;

- a professional friend who witnesses to Jesus Christ, the revelation of God's friendship of suffering and liberating love with humankind, with a community of collegial friends whose object (aim) is the increasing freedom of God's friendship with humankind.

Therefore, each function is exercised by a minister-friend with other ordained and non-ordained friends who are also called to ministry for the purpose of witnessing to Jesus Christ, the revelation of God's friendship of suffering and liberating love with humankind, all done toward the end of increasing the freedom of God's friendship with humankind. Properly understood, each function of the model is exercised by a friend, with friends, who witness to friendship, for the freedom of friendship.

In Relationship to Communal Disciplined Practices

What follows are a few snapshots taken within a public community. Starting to develop is a more composite picture of the model in operation.

All of the functions of ministry seek to build, nurture and guide a Christian community in which friends can engage in certain communal disciplined practices that can be understood and experienced, by action of the Holy Spirit, as means of grace. A contemporary list of such communal disciplined practices could include:

- worshiping God together—praising God, giving thanks for God's creative and redemptive work in the world, hearing God's word preached and receiving the sacraments given to us in Christ;

- telling the Christian story to one another—reading and hearing the Scriptures and also the stories of the church's experience throughout its history;

- interpreting together the Scriptures and the history of the church's experience, particularly in relation to their meaning for our own lives in the world;

- praying—together and by ourselves, not only in formal services of worship, but in all times and places;

- confessing our sin to one another, and forgiving and becoming reconciled with one another;

- tolerating one another's failures and encouraging one another in the work each must do and the vocation each must live;

- carrying out specific faithful acts of service and witness together;

- suffering with and for each other and all whom Jesus showed us to be our neighbors;

- providing hospitality and care, not only to one another but to strangers;

- listening and talking attentively to one another about our particular experiences in life;

- struggling together to become conscious of and understand the nature of the context in which we live;

- criticizing and resisting all those powers and patterns (both within the church and in the world as a whole) that destroy human beings, corrode human community, and injure God's creation;

- working together to maintain and create social structures and institutions which will sustain life in the world in ways that accord with God's will. (Dykstra:27-28)

There is a positive correlation among all the functions and all the communal disciplined practices. All of them are interdependent with and mutually reinforcing of one another. When one function and/or practice is underdeveloped, all are weakened. When one function and/or practice is strengthened, all are strengthened.

There is no one-to-one relationship between the different functions of ministry and the set of communal disciplined practices.

Rather, every form of ministry is responsible for doing its part to establish and sustain the whole complex of practices. Likewise, every form of ministry is itself some constellation of all of the practices. Thus, every one of these practices should contribute to every form of ministry, and every form of ministry must work to sustain and relate to each other the whole variety of practices. . . . Practically speaking, the adequacy of a form of ministry can be evaluated in part by the degree to which all of these practices are involved in and sustained by that form of ministry. When some are missing, an evaluation of the way in which that ministry is being carried out may well be called for. For as each of the practices is increasingly built into every form of ministry and as the quality of the community's active participation in the practices is enhanced and enriched in and by that form of ministry, the one ministry of the whole church is itself made stronger. (Dykstra:31-32)

In Relationship to Faith

While there is a causal relationship between the functions and the practices, as well as between the practices and the functions, there is none between faith. There is neither a causal connection between the functions and faith, nor a causal connection between the communal disciplined practices and faith. Faith is a gift from God. However, in spite of this lack of causality concerning faith, the functions build-nurture-guide the communal disciplined practices and the communal disciplined practices build-nurture-guide the functions. The functions and the disciplined practices together build-nurture-guide a community of friends who participate in the functions and the disciplined practices. By their participation, the public community of friends also help to build-nurture-guide a communal context in which, by the power of the Holy Spirit, persons may come to faith and grow in faith and the life of faith.

In Relationship to Society

All of this may seem too cozy for authentic comfort or too threatening for authentic challenge, yet neither charge is totally accurate. Additionally, the needs of the world may seem to have been forgotten. Such is not the case. A mediating community can begin to minister to many persons. It is an energizing *milieu,* which literally translates as *"mi"* meaning "middle" and *"lieu"* meaning "place" and, therefore, denotes a "middle-place." A mediating community is a "middle-place" between the potentially asphyxiating personality of a lifestyle enclave and the potentially asphyxiating impersonality of a megastructure. This public community begins to experience and to mediate new meaning, the value of unique belonging and creative direction through moral investigation, discussion and general consensus.

However, meaning, value, and direction are not identical to Christian faith. Here Dykstra, again in his *Growing in the Life of Christian Faith*, gives pertinent counsel.

> . . . [I]t is a mistake to identify Christian faith with a way of making sense out of life, with a way of finding meaning, direction, and value in it. Faith and the life of faith are indeed seen and experienced by Christians as filled with meaning, value, and life direction that is ultimately trustworthy and true. The God known in faith is the overflowing reservoir of all that is valuable and good. And to live "according to the Spirit," to live "in Christ," is to be placed in intimate contact with that God in every dimension of our lives. But meaning and faith are not the same. Meaning, value, and direction are neither the substance, the aim, nor the means of faith and the life of faith. Rather, they are by-products.
>
> In the experience of faith and the life of faith, a transformation takes place. Meaning, value, and life direction all become relativized. They are no longer the prize we seek. In Christ, our very hungers become transformed, so that to live in Christ is the only food we crave. In Christ, we are free to give up all else—even meaning, value, direction, and our search for them. For they are not God. The surprise, however, is that in being free to give them up we find them returned to us a hundred-fold. Just as those who lose their lives for Christ's sake gain them back (Matt. 16:25), so also do those who, in Christ, let loose of their strivings for meaning, value, and direction gain them all back again, but indirectly, as a gift, and different in kind from that which they had expected, from that for which they had hoped. (18-19)

While meaning, value, and direction are not identical to Christian faith, nevertheless, meaning, value and direction are deep needs within society and church that can be met abundantly in the life of faith within and by a public community of friends. These friends witness—in attitude, word, and deed—to Jesus Christ, who is the revelation of God's friendship of suffering and liberating love with humankind.

The friendship model of ministry as a contemporary sociological mediating structure envisions a dynamic friendship between the ministerial functions, the communal disciplined practices, a public community of friends, global society, God, a context in which faith may be gifted and nurtured and a transformed sense of meaning, value and direction.

Notes

1. I owe my formal introduction to this ingredient of friendship to Moltmann (1977:316): " . . . The *congregatio sanctorum* . . . is really the fellowship of friends who live in the friendship of Jesus and spread friendliness in the fellowship, by meeting the forsaken with affection and the despised with respect."

2. With lines from Tocqueville (1969:512-513), Bellah (1985:174) draws an interesting course of action: [The bracketed amendments to the following quotation of Tocqueville have been added. They do not appear in Bellah].

> . . . Tocqueville thought that such a vision of the public good founded in enlightened self-interest was "the best suited of all philosophical theories to the wants of [persons] in our time." It did "not inspire great sacrifices, but every day it prompts some small ones; by itself it cannot make a [person] virtuous, but its discipline shapes a lot of orderly, temperate, moderate, careful, and self-controlled citizens." . . . But as Tocqueville noted, such civic virtues were not purely and simply the product of interest calculations. Enlightened self-interest established "habits" that "unconsciously" turned the will toward such virtues. "At first it is by necessity that [persons] attend to the public interest, afterward by choice. What had been calculation becomes instinct. By dint of working for the good of [one's] fellow citizens, [one] in the end acquires a habit and taste for serving them."

3. For a more detailed sociological description of contemporary culture, see Berger (1977:70-80) chapter 6, "Toward a Critique of Modernity." Here Berger catalogues the following elements of modernity: "abstraction," "futurity," "individuation," "liberation," and "secularization."

4. This list of the characteristics of a public community is adapted from a class lecture given by Dr. Douglas W. Hix of Columbia Theological Seminary of Decatur, Georgia in a Doctor of Ministry course called "Seminar on Ministry," Winter-Spring 1990. See also Berger (1977:130-141).

5. This spread of opportunities is adapted from Professor Hix's previously noted seminar.

6. These notations are also adapted from Dr. Hix's seminar.

7. Empty individualism is that which has as its loci an empty self. An empty self does not operate out of self-integrating elements. An empty self is a vacuous self which operates out of the vacuum of constantly changing, self-abortive elements. Bellah and his co-authors (1985:154) place "the empty self" and "the constituted self" at the opposite ends of an analytic continuum:

> The empty self . . . is an analytic concept, a limit toward which we tend, but not a concrete reality. A completely empty self could not exist except in the theory of radical individualism. It is theoretically imaginable but performatively impossible. The constituted self is also an analytic concept, a limit that is never quite reached. It is true that we are all children of specific parents, born in a particular locality, inheritors of those group histories, and citizens of this nation. All of these things tell us who we are in important ways. But we live in a society that encourages us to cut free from the past, to define our own selves, to choose the groups with which we wish to identify. No tradition and no community in the United States is above criticism, and the test of the criticism is usually the degree to which the community or tradition helps the individual to find fulfillment. So we live somewhere between the empty and the constituted self.

> For help in clarifying the terms "individualism," "ontological individualism," "expressive individualism," and "utilitarian individualism," the following sections are quoted in their entirety from Bellah (1985:333-336) in the "Glossary of Some Key Terms."

> *Individualism.* A word used in numerous, sometimes contradictory, senses. We use it mainly in two: (1) a belief in the inherent dignity and, indeed, sacredness of the human person. In this sense, individualism is part of all four of the American traditions we have described in this book—biblical, republican, utilitarian individualism, and expressive individualism; (2) a belief that the individual has a primary reality whereas society is a second-order, derived or artificial construct, a view we call *ontological individualism.* This view is shared by utilitarian and expressive individualists. It is opposed to the view that society is as real as individuals, a view we call *social realism,* which is common to the biblical and republican traditions . . .

> *Expressive individualism.* Expressive individualism holds that each person has a unique core of feeling and intuition that should unfold or be expressed if individuality is to be realized. This core, though unique, is not necessarily alien to other persons or to nature. Under certain

conditions, the expressive individualist may find it possible through intuitive feeling to "merge" with other persons, with nature, or with the cosmos as a whole. Expressive individualism is related to the phenomenon of romanticism in eighteenth and nineteenth-century European and American culture. In the twentieth century, it shows affinities with the culture of psychotherapy . . .

Utilitarian individualism. A form of individualism that takes as given certain basic human appetites and fears—for Hobbes, the desire for power over others and the fear of sudden violent death at the hands of another—and sees human life as an effort by individuals to maximize their self-interest relative to these given ends. Utilitarian individualism views society as arising from a contract that individuals enter into only in order to advance their self-interest. According to Locke, society is necessary because of the prior existence of property, the protection of which is the reason individuals contractually enter society. Utilitarian individualism has an affinity to a basically economic understanding of human existence. . .

8. See Niebuhr (1977:48-49) chapter 2, "The Emerging New Conception of the Ministry."

9. This chart was given as a class handout for the previously cited Doctor of Ministry course.

10. It may be interesting to think of Niebuhr's sociological-theological-pastoral chart as descriptions throughout history of the Church's credence table, from which it has conducted its ministry.

11. Although Niebuhr's analysis deals only with ministerial models since the time of Gregory the Great, I profess the existence of the "church" with its "ministry" as the faith community in the Old Testament. Furthermore, I am in agreement with Alston (1984:9-15) when he cites a good case for claiming that the church begins with creation.

Chapter III

The Friendship Model of Ministry as a Normative Theological Mediating Structure

Now there is an examination of the friendship model of ministry as a normative theological mediating structure in relationship to a concept of limitation, authority, Jesus' ministry and change.

In Relationship to a Concept of Limitation

A model of ministry is also a model of theology. Thus, several disclaimers are in order at the start of the theological exploration.

In the first place, it is confessed that the normative[1] theological tradition obviously exerts a powerful influence upon the model and its theology. For most of the model's components, there is specific and deep indebtedness to other persons. Yet, the initial conception and arrangement of the model are products of the imagination,[2] augmented by personal, theological, ecclesiastical and societal reflection—all gratefully done within the historical and living tradition of a nurturing community. Nonetheless, in no way is radical creativity claimed.

Secondly, it is conceded that God does not work exclusively with and through the church. God is also active outside the church with and without the church's assistance. It is because of the nature of this book that the church looms so large.

Thirdly, it is conceived that God may not be interested singularly in humankind, or even primarily interested in humankind (Gustafson:87-

113).[3] Yet, in the glow of the incarnation, life, death, resurrection and promised return of Christ, it can be said that it appears that God is at least significantly concerned with humankind.

Fourthly, it is acknowledged that, for several reasons, this chapter is in no respect a detailed theological excursus. a. The theological content is limited. We do not know everything about ourselves; much less do we know everything about God. God transcends our understanding. Accordingly, this is not the theology of the model of the ministry. It is a theory of a theology of a model of a ministry. b. The theological scope is limited. The model endorses friendship. It is evident, however, that the created world includes many other forms of life other than human and includes many other important issues, such as those of global stewardship and planetary hygiene. While other issues and other life forms are not specifically addressed in the model and its theology, a *tableau* of divine and human friendship can imply nurturing friendly relationships with the earth and its creatures and natural resources, and imaginatively can be projected to a universal friendship of *shalom* with God and all of creation (Daley and Cobb:376-400).[4] c. The theological design is limited. It does not begin to approach being definitive. The design of the model's selective discussion of a theology is only an inkling.

In Relationship to a Concept of Authority

After disclaiming, there is proclaiming.

The concept of authority that is attested to in the friendship model of ministry as a normative theological mediating structure is an authority of *witness*. Hendrikus Berkhof gives a tantalizing introduction to his biblical study of "Witnesses."

> A frequent use of the word 'witness' and its derivatives belongs to the ecclesiastical and ecumenical fashion of today. I wonder whether its verbal frequency is matched by its existential frequency or whether the first is a sign of the lack of the second. In both cases we have good reason to welcome the emphasis upon the dimension of witnessing in the life of the Church and of the individual member. This usage in the church jargon of today falls, however, far behind its biblical usage. Compared with the biblical meaning, we have individualized and institutionalized the word. We understand it mainly as a function and expression of . . . [one's] private conviction or as one of the duties on the

programmes of the churches. In the Bible, witness has a far wider
context and far more dimensions than we have been accustomed to
see. We shall try to indicate some of these dimensions. (1964:98)[5]

The concept of authority that is attested to in the friendship model of
ministry as a normative theological mediating structure is a *trinitarian*
authority of witness. Here Berkhof introduces the teamwork of expert
witnesses.

> *The trinitarian dimension.* This is particularly evident in the Gospel
> and the Epistles of John. In general, it can be said that no biblical
> tradition is more aware of the basic significance of witness than the
> Johannine one. Here the original witness is God the Father himself.
> Jesus says: "The Father who sent me has himself borne witness to me"
> (5.37; cf. 5.32; 8.3-18; I John 5.9). As the Father bears witness to
> Christ, so does Christ to the Father, because he testifies to what he has
> seen and heard (3.11, 32f.). He came into the world to bear witness to
> the truth (18.37). So he is "the faithful and true witness" (Rev. 1.5;
> 3.14), and that not only by his words but also by water and the blood
> (I John 5.8; i.e., by his baptism and his death) and by being the first-
> born of the dead (Rev. 1.5). The Father and the Son witness together:
> "I bear witness to myself and the Father who sent me bears witness to
> me" (John 8.18). The continuation and application of this twofold wit-
> ness is the testimony of the Spirit: "The Spirit is the witness because
> the Spirit is the truth" (I John 5.7), "He will bear witness to me"
> (15.26; cf. 16.8 and 13), "It is the Spirit himself bearing witness with
> our spirit that we are children of God" (Rom. 8.16). Witness is prima-
> rily a trinitarian work, a divine, not a human work. Primarily, but not
> exclusively! For . . . (humankind] is invited and enabled to participate
> in this trinitarian activity: "The Spirit will bear witness to me, and you
> also are witnesses" (John 15.26f.; cf. I John 5.10). We too share in
> this—in full dependence, however, on the divine witness of the Son:
> "For the testimony of Jesus (about himself) is the spirit of (our) proph-
> ecy" (Rev. 19.10); and also in full dependence on the Spirit: "for it is
> not you who speak but the Spirit of your Father speaking through you"
> (Matt. 10.18). (1964:98-99)

The concept of authority that is attested to in the friendship model of
ministry as a normative theological mediating structure is a trinitarian
juridical authority of witness. There is a kind of juridical dimension to
the trinitarian authority of witness, yet in no way is it legalistic. The
authority of witness is not the witness of authority. The analogue of the

trinitarian juridical authority of witness is not biblically inconsequential. Again Berkhof makes the point.

> *The juridical dimension.* This is closely related to the . . . [trinitarian dimension of witness]. Markus Barth in his book, *The Eye-witness,* says: "The concept of witness and the similar concepts . . . stem from the realm of juridical life" (p. 272). The late Theo Preiss has written a small but extremely thoughtful study on the juridical concept in the Gospel of John,[1] in which he proves that the so-called "mystical" Gospel of John is full of juridical terminology. Particularly the verb *marturein,* which is more frequent in the Johannine writings than in all the other New Testament books put together, has a juridical meaning. The witness to the mighty acts of God in Jesus Christ cannot be a question of mere personal conviction or even of individual sentiment. It has to meet the strictest standards of validity, because "the witness is part of the evidence." It can meet these standards because this witness bears the highest truth. A basic biblical and rabbinic rule for the validity of a testimony is contained in Deut. 19.15: "Only on the evidence of two witnesses or of three witnesses shall a charge be sustained." Jesus mentions it in relation to what I have called the trinitarian dimension of witness (John 8.17). It is quoted several times in the New Testament. Even more interesting is the fact that the New Testament witnesses act upon this rule either explicitly or silently.[2] Jesus sent out his disciples two by two (Mark 6.7). I John 5.8 says: "There are three witnesses, the Spirit, the water and the blood; and these three agree." In Revelation 11, two witnesses are sent to prophesy for one thousand two hundred and sixty days. Two women saw the resurrected Lord (Matt. 28.1) or three (according to Mark 16.3). Two disciples saw him according to John (20.2). Two others, going to Emmaus, were accompanied by him (Luke 24.13ff.). Paul is particularly interested in the juridical validity of the testimony to the resurrection, enumerating many witnesses, "most of whom are still alive" . . . (I Cor. 15.6). (1964:100-101)[6]

The concept of authority that is attested to in the friendship model of ministry as a normative theological mediating structure is a trinitarian juridical authority of witness that has formal and material authority. It also ultimately agrees formally and materially. In the normative theological tradition, there are three essential visions of God: a *Patermartus* vision of God, an *Uiosmartus* vision of God and a *Pneumamartus* vision of God. A *Patermartus* vision of God denotes *pater* (father) plus *martus* (witness) which connotes a *Patermartus* (father-witness) vision; similarly, an *Uiosmartus* vision of God denotes *uios* (son) plus *martus* (witness) which connotes an *Uiosmartus* (son-witness) vision; and finally, a *Pneumamartus* vision of God denotes *pneuma* (spirit) plus *martus* (witness) which connotes a *Pneumamartus* (spirit-witness) vision.

The Greek words *pater* and *uios* are obviously of the masculine gender. While in *Koine* Greek *pneuma* is of the neuter gender, considering the broader history of its connotative meanings, even *pneuma* is not generic. One can find numerous historical and contemporary examples of *pneuma* being used (implicitly or explicitly) in either the feminine gender, the masculine gender, as well as in the neuter gender. Therefore, it is clear that of course *pater* and *uios,* but also even *pneuma* do not consistently connote neutral, non-prejudicial meanings. It is even more evident that all of the theological traditions for which these terms have been invoked are not unbiased. So, why then use these terms? The Greek word *martus* (witness) is employed because it is consonant with and important to the model's theology. But, why use the forced terms of the *Patermartus* vision of God, plus the *Uiosmartus* vision of God, plus the *Pneumamartus* vision of God in order to comprise the trinity-witness vision of God? A weak answer to that question is now given: instead of the English words for father-son-spirit, their Greek equivalent is adopted at this juncture as an elementary attempt toward a way of not consciously and automatically legitimating *en masse* the historical and contemporary hierarchicalism, imperialism, and patriarchalism of both the Church and society. Later on in the discussion, the traditional English terms will be used, but not in the sense of consciously endorsing hierarchicalism, imperialism, and patriarchalism.

However, a trivial change of words in this case changes very little, if anything, and the present writer remains biased, as do all human beings. There is no such category of existence, at least in this life, as unbiased experience. There is no unbiased contexuality.[7] Our contexuality at whatever level—categorical or mundane—is our bias, and our bias is our contexuality. Instead of feebly referring to four common *Koine* words, maybe a more honest, serious and proactive perspective would continually ask and seek to answer at least three questions—in the active contexuality of exercising the communal disciplined practices: 1. To what extent is our bias recognized, in its categorical sense and in its multitude of legionnaire expressions?; 2. How open are we to have our categorical bias and its existential pluralities engaged in radical dialogue?; and 3. Are we willing to have our bias completely contradicted?

Now we come back to the trialogue of authority that is attested to in the friendship model of ministry as a normative theological mediating structure. It is a trinitarian juridical authority of witness that has formal and material authority, and also ultimately agrees formally and materially. The normative theological tradition gives witness to the three essential visions of God: a *Patermartus* vision, an *Uiosmartus* vision, and a *Pneumamartus* vision. There are real distinctions within and among the *Patermartus* vision, the *Uiosmartus* vision, and the *Pneumamartus* vision. Yet, it is not legitimate to play one vision against another. There is also a real unity within and among each vision. Ultimately, each vision corresponds to and with each other vision and together the combined trinitarian witness constitutes a truer theocentric vision than any one of the visions can contribute individually.[8] Ultimately, the trinitarian juridical authority of witness is the witness of the formal and material agreement of an ultimate collaborative consensus.

The concept of authority that is attested to in the friendship model of ministry as a normative theological mediating structure is a trinitarian juridical authority of witness that has, in addition to formal and material authority, functional authority. Likewise, in addition to formal and material agreement, it also agrees functionally. The external formal, material and functional trinitarian juridical authority of witness is *for the sake of the world*. Berkhof explores the cosmic dimension of witness.

> *The cosmic dimension.* The trinitarian witness is directed towards the world. God is involved in a trial with the gods and with the evil one. In that trial . . . [God] wants to "convince the world" (John 16.8). An impressive vision of that cosmic trial we find in Isaiah 43 and 44, especially in 43.8-11, where the Lord in front of the nations challenges the idols "to bring their witnesses to justify them" (9). To Israel he says: "You are my witnesses," because they can testify by experience to . . . [God's] faithfulness in . . . [God's] acts of judgment and deliverance. In the midst of a world partly full of gods and partly without any god, God's people have to deliver the demonstration of the Spirit and of power. I believe that Jesus' words in Acts 1.8: "You shall be my witnesses," contain an allusion to the words in Isaiah 43 and 44. He also calls his disciples to testify in his favour in the great cosmic trial. John 16 uses a similar terminology, where the Spirit in this trial is the public prosecutor of the world and at the same time the advocate of the faithful. (1964:99-100)

The concept of authority that is attested to in the friendship model of ministry as a normative theological mediating structure is a trinitarian juridical authority of witness for the sake of the world. This witness suggests a pattern for a theology. This witness also suggests a pattern for constructing a world view. Indeed, theology can be imagined to be a way of construing a world view (Gustafson:158-163).[9] The trinitarian juridical authority of witness for the sake of the world suggests both something of a theology and a world view, or a hint of a theological world view. Hence, a normative Christian theology can construe a trinitarian theocentric world view with Christ at the center, mediated by the Holy Spirit for the sake of the world. This is an interpretation of a normative Christian understanding of the revelation of God.

However, in another sense, there is nothing normative about the revelation of God. The term "revelation of God" is vague and undifferentiated.[10] A manner by which to begin to conceptualize this phrase is to make a basic distinction between revelation of God as being "revelation from God about," and revelation of God as being "revelation from God of." The former is the revelation of knowledge; the latter is the revelation of presence. Revelation of God can connote and denote the presence of knowledge and/or the knowledge of presence. The revelation of God can mean the revelation from God about knowledge. This is the presence of true knowledge. The revelation of God can also mean the revelation from God of presence. This is the knowledge of true presence. Thus, the revelation of God can mean the presence of revealed knowledge, and the revelation of God can mean the knowledge of revealed presence. Furthermore, both distinctions of the revelation of God are equated with truth. The revelation of God as the presence of revealed knowledge is truth. The revelation of God as the knowledge of revealed presence is truth. Both senses of the revelation of God are truth identifications. The presence of revealed knowledge is the truth of knowledge. The knowledge of revealed presence is the truth of presence. The revelation of God intimates at least two basic distinctions: 1. the revelation of God as the truth of revealed knowledge; and 2. the revelation of God as the truth of revealed presence.

Yet, this dual attempt to differentiate the revelation of God is ambiguous, as is also the fact that there are many different and seemingly conflicting biblical descriptions of revelation. Consequently, the terms "revelation of God" and "word of God" remain quite vague. Given even Barth's illuminating threefold description of the word of God (1975:88-

124), both terms in themselves and in their relation to one another need more clarity.[11] The concept of the word of God does not grant greater precision to the concept of the revelation of God: it is the other way around. A biblically congruent concept of the revelation of God serves well as the superintending principle of the concept of the word of God (Pannenberg:256-257). While the following conjecture is highly speculative, is only embryonic and is unaccompanied by an exegetical basis, yet, it is still presented as a neonatal notion toward further distinction of and between the concept of the revelation of God and the concept of the word of God.[12]

The revelation of God is equal to the past, present and future historical saving action of God. As such, the revelation of God is also identical to either one or the other or both of the following actions that can be distinguished but not divided: 1. the presence of the divinely revealed historical saving knowledge of truth and/or of God, which is the word of God; and 2. the knowledge of the divinely revealed historical saving presence of God, which is the Spirit of God.[13] Both of these expressions of revelation are ultimately witnessed to in the saving history of Jesus Christ, who is both the Word of God incarnate and the Spirit of God incarnate. Conceived of as a composite whole, the revelation of God (which also implies the hiddenness of God) is the past, present and future historical saving action of the trinitarian God, with Christ as the revelatory center, mediated by the Holy Spirit for the sake of the world.

The past, present and future historical saving action of God is a process of revealed intimacy, the intimacy of truth: the intimate truth of divinely revealed historical saving knowledge and the intimate truth of divinely revealed historical saving presence. Therefore, Christian theology interprets and appropriates the revelation of God in both of its intimated distinctions. Christian theology interprets and appropriates what it perceives as, trusts as and obeys as the revelation of God; or, it can be said that Christian theology interprets and appropriates what it believes to be, receives as and responds to as the revelation of God. The circularity of all of this is not denied. In reality, theology interprets what it interprets to be the revelation of God; or, it construes what it construes to be the revelation of God. Only in this way does theology appropriate the revelation of God, which is the intimate witness of true revealed knowledge and the intimate witness of true revealed presence, both of which are part of the witnessing activity of God.[14] Christian theology appropriates the trinitarian theocentric revelation-witness of God with

Christ at the center, mediated by the Holy Spirit for the sake of the world by the process of a threefold reference to penultimate authorities of witness. Thereby, theology constructs its world view. These penultimate authorities of witness have, upon occasion throughout the history of God's friendship with humankind, falsely claimed a position of authority that rightly resides only in God's ultimate authoritative historical saving act of revelation in Jesus Christ. The penultimate authorities of witness are the primary source of the witness of the Bible, the secondary source of the witness of tradition and the tertiary source of the witness of personal experience.[15]

As one may have come to expect, Berkhof also gives a particularly instructive introduction to the witness of personal experience in relationship to revelation. The beginning of his section, "Revelation and Experience," is a pertinent synopsis.

> If revelation is always linked with earthly experiences, while yet, in virtue of its nature, it transcends it, the relationship of revelation and experience is an issue that is bound to come to the forefront time and again. Such is especially the case in our time, in which our experience of reality is so secularized that many can hardly conceive of experience as providing access to revelation. The fact that experience is a vague term that regularly causes confusion makes the investigation even more difficult. In the study of faith it legitimately comes up for discussion in three ways: 1. as experience that precedes the revelational encounter and leads up to it; 2. as another term for the faith encounter itself; 3. as designation of personal experiences and experiences with the world that are evoked by the faith encounter. . . . (1986:55)

In the theology of the friendship model of ministry as a normative theological mediating structure, experience is implied or applied only in the above first and third sense. However, experience in the second sense seems to be endorsed by the previous presentation of the three sources of an authority of witness: scripture, tradition, and personal experience. Also, this brief presentation does not adequately describe the role of personal experience in scripture and tradition. Personal experience is a boggling entanglement. Although more talk will not divest personal experience of its confusing complexity, still more attention needs to be given to the term "personal experience."

Therefore, the model's theology envisions personal experience and the penultimate witnesses to revelation in the following manner. A more accurate conception of the three penultimate sources of an authority of witness would present these relative authorities as being: 1. the personal experience and interpretation of scripture; 2. the personal experience and interpretation of tradition; and 3. the personal experience and inter- pretation of personal experience (or existential being). In no sense is personal experience (either in and of scripture, in and of tradition, or in and of existential being) a direct point of contact to revelation. The faith statement is also made that in no sense is personal experience (either in and of scripture, in and of tradition, or in and of existential being) equal to revelation. Yet, all revelation is received through some form of per- sonal experience, that is, through some form of an intersubjective-social network. When personal experience is perceived epistemologically as an existential hermeneutical principle, then it can also be perceived that there is no im-mediate (without mediation) revelation, and that there is no im-personal (without person) revelation. The only authentic point of contact to revelation, the revelation-witness of God, is the Holy Spirit, who is still nonetheless not directly received, but who is only received through some form of personal experience. Revelation in the model's theology may involve what may be understood to be insight and inspira- tion in relationship to the three sources of an authority of witness; but revelation is neither directly accessed by, nor is it identical to, such insight and inspiration that may be emergent from the three sources of an authority of witness. Rather, the truth claim is made that revelation is the past, present and future historical saving action of God, who can never in this life be encountered directly. The revelation-witness of God in Christ can only be received through the mediation of the Holy Spirit, who is also only mediated through some form of personal experience. There is no immediate, impersonal experience of the revelation of God— either in the sense of being the truth of revealed knowledge, or in the sense of being the truth of revealed presence. There is no non-experien- tial experience of the revelation of God (Barth, 1957:57).[16]

The revelation-witness of God in Christ through the witness of the Holy Spirit implies not only a mediating principle, but also implies a manifesting principle. The Holy Spirit mediates-manifests Jesus Christ. Through Jesus Christ, the Holy Spirit mediates-manifests the trinitarian witness. The Holy Spirit mediates-manifests the trinitarian witness as it may be encountered, in a qualified sense, in the witness of scripture, in the witness of tradition and in the witness of personal experience.

In addition to the principle of mediation and the principle of manifestation, the witness of the Holy Spirit (as well as the trinitarian witness) implies a principle of authentication. There is a principle of mediation, a principle of manifestation and a principle of authentication that is implied in the witness of the person and work of each agent of the trinity. All three principles are formally, materially and functionally interrelated. All three principles are also formally, materially and functionally interrelated within and among each agent of the trinitarian witness in general, as well as in the trinitarian revelation-witness in particular.[17]

This mediating-manifesting-authenticating principle that is implied in the witnessing activity of the trinity is what the model's theology imagines when it speaks about the concept of "an authority of witness" in relationship to the trinitarian vision, scripture, tradition and personal experience. However, this construel neither posits the mediating-manifesting-authenticating principle into the trinitarian vision, into any biblical, traditional, or personal vision, into scripture, into tradition or into personal experience; nor does this construel make such a deposit into any single vision or witness, or collective vision or witness of penultimate sources. The penultimate visions or sources of an authority of witness do not possess intrinsically any manifest or latent mediating-manifesting-authenticating power that, apart from the Holy Spirit's work, is sufficiently, perspicuously and efficaciously authoritative. Yet, the penultimate sources of scripture, tradition and personal experience (from which is "appropriated" the trinitarian vision) can become a source of an authority of witness by virtue of, and only by virtue of, the mediating-manifesting-authenticating activity of the Holy Spirit.

Thus, the hermeneutical process can be construed further. The Holy Spirit mediates-manifests-authenticates the revelation-witness of the person and work of Jesus Christ. Through Jesus Christ, the Holy Spirit also mediates-manifests-authenticates the revelation-witness of the person and work of each agent of the trinity as follows: as the revelation-witness of God may be encountered in the mediating-manifesting-authenticating activity of the Holy Spirit in the personal experience and interpretation of the witness of scripture; as the revelation-witness of God may be encountered in the mediating-manifesting-authenticating activity of the Holy Spirit in the personal experience and interpretation of the witness of tradition; and as the revelation-witness of God may be encountered in the mediating-manifesting-authenticating activity of the Holy Spirit in the personal experience and interpretation of the witness of personal experience. This convoluted imaging of the hermeneutical process is sketched for the purpose of being one way to avoid, at least consciously, some of the more blatant errors of biblicism, traditionalism and spiritualism.

Biblicistical, traditionalistical and spiritualistical errors are those which fail to see not only that the term personal experience is a confounding conundrum, but these errors also fail to see that all three penultimate sources of an authority of witness are complexly interrelated.[18] Furthermore, (the sense is repeated) it is a categorical given that there always exists an experimenter's bias.

> . . . [I]t is clear that one's place is history, society, culture, and even nature affects what is seen, and how what is seen is construed. There is no possibility of human emancipation from the particularities of a perspective. (Gustafson:300-301)

Not only is there an experimenter's bias, the whole experiment itself is biased. The experiment of interpretation always involves a biased experimenter (interpreter) biasly experimenting with (interpreting) biased experimental datum (scripture-tradition-personal experience). There is no such experience as unbiased presuppositionless exegesis of unbiased presuppositionless scripture; there is no such experience as unbiased presuppositionless exegesis of unbiased presuppositionless tradition; and there is no such experience as unbiased presuppositionless exegesis of unbiased presuppositionless personal experience.

The reality of being inextricably entangled with and tricked by the minions of biased human perception does not automatically reduce theology to trifling, narcissistic nonsense. There are three normative guides which coordinate the theological examination of the three penultimate sources of an authority of witness. Gordon Kaufman, through his *Systematic Theology*, administers an insightful survey of the entire interpretive enterprise.

> . . . [T]here is the historical norm: what we take to be God's decisive act should correspond for our time to what the Christian community of other generations has known it to be . . . [T]here is the experiential norm: our theology must make sense of our own experience, of the world we live in . . . [And there is] the systematic [norm]: the various aspects and dimensions, doctrines and dogmas, of Christian faith must be developed and displayed in their interconnection with and implication of each other, with the whole carefully disciplined methodologically. (75-78)

The formal systematic norm may not be currently in dominant vogue. In spite of this possible fashion, even non-systematic works of limited treatment flex to be systematic in their circumspected field. So, it is still instructive to interpret the three sources of an authority of witness with reference to the three normative guidelines.

> . . . The three norms of theological thinking outlined here appear . . . to be criteria which are operative in various ways in every theologian's thinking: each is seeking to speak with contemporary relevance, in faithfulness to God's revelation in history, and consistently. If we consciously and explicitly distinguish these dimensions, developing criteria appropriate to each, our theological thinking should more truly apprehend and reflect God's act and more significantly illuminate human existence. But the difficulty of the task should always be kept in view: it will never reach finality or completion; there is always more to be done. Theology remains forever a demand as well as an achievement. (Kaufman:78-79)

The theological experiment is afforded no seal of certitude or closure. Nonetheless, there can be found some measure of assurance about having approximated the norms of history, experience and coherence within an intelligible "system" that constructs a world view with the trifocal lenses of an authority of witness. There can also be found some measure of treasure that is contiguous with the contours of the risky mission of interpretation.

> Relying on the Holy Spirit, who opens our eyes and hearts, we affirm our freedom to interpret Scripture responsibly. God has chosen to address his inspired Word to us through diverse and varied human writings. Therefore we use the best available methods to understand them in their historical and cultural settings and the literary forms in which they are cast. When we encounter apparent tensions and conflicts in what Scripture teaches us to believe and do, the final appeal must be to the authority of Christ. Acknowledging that authority, comparing Scripture with Scripture, listening with respect to fellow-believers past and present, we anticipate that the Holy Spirit will enable us to interpret faithfully God's Word for our time and place. (Presbyterian Publishing House:169)

It is admirable to exercise *ex animo* such faithful anticipation and conscientious interpretation of the three sources of an authority of witness in consistent dialogue with the three normative guidelines. However, simultaneously, the trekking theologian confesses all along the way that motives and intentions and perspectives remain muddled. Working toward more clarity, the diligent interpreter can decide to proceed as defenselessly as is humanly possible, so that nothing need be precluded from purview. Yet, even in the climate of avowed, open investigation, there can be a covert activity which unconsciously sneaks to conform revelation to the substandard of scripture, tradition, personal experience, or some combination thereof. It is a ruinous rut.

In order to attempt to shift the direction of such a clandestine operation, one can consciously work toward and pray toward having one's personal experience and interpretation of scripture, one's personal experience and interpretation of tradition, and one's personal experience and interpretation of existential being—all illuminated and transformed by the revelation of God. In the seemingly wild and potentially radical hope of such a redemptive transformation, one may work toward and pray for the mediating-manifesting-authenticating activity of the Holy Spirit, who verifies the trinitarian authority of witness as interpreted through the truth of Jesus Christ, the truth of whom is also verified by the Holy Spirit as attested to in scripture, resonated in tradition, echoed in personal experience and meaningfully collated in culture—all clarified within the communal disciplined practices.

However, no clarification is ever given a final stamp of inerrant authenticity. Only God's revelation is the ultimate canon, of which God alone is the absolute judge. Therefore, theology can never accomplish infallibly the arduous and ambiguous interpretive assignment. It can, nevertheless, encounter a revelatory event and can encounter revelatory events, upon which is constructed a Christian world view. Again, Kaufman is revealing.

> An event is "revelatory," . . . if it is itself apprehended as meaningful and throws its light on other dark and obscure aspects of experience as well. No revelatory event is of ultimate or decisive significance, however, unless through it comes the meaning that illuminates all our existence, giving us means to understand even the most elusive corner of ourselves and our world. If the Christ-event is to be grasped as God's definitive revelatory act, it must be seen as illumining every dimension of self and world. In its light we should be able to understand more adequately the problems of personal existence (guilt, fear, despair, meaninglessness, moral problems, difficulties of personal decision);

the problems of our society (war, racial tensions, depersonalization, automation); the problems of our intellectual life (issues raised by "the scientific world-view," by the social sciences, philosophy, and psychology); the problems of modern culture (the role of the artist in contemporary society, the significance of the great historical movements of our time, the meaning of human history as a whole). Only as these various facets of our actual existence are illumined by God's act in Christ, can we say that it really is revelation to us and for us.

Theology must [therefore] attend to and be prepared to analyze political and economic developments, scientific and philosophical theory, communal and religious practices, works of art and literature, everyday personal and social experience—everything that contributes to the stuff of human existence must be brought under the revelatory light. Since the Christian Gospel is good news about the human situation as such, and thus about every dimension of life, no aspect of existence is too insignificant or too remote to be of theological interest. As these multifarious materials are exposed to and measured by the standard of reality and meaning emergent from the revelatory event, the theologian seeks to interpret and evaluate the several dimensions of experience so as to produce a genuinely Christian perspective on life and the world. (73-74)

Therefore, the perspective of the model constructs a world view and a model of trinitarian theology and *praxis* which witnesses to Christ as the revelatory center (Frie:1975), mediated-manifested-authenticated by the Holy Spirit for the sake of the world. Jesus Christ—fully God, fully human—is the unique and normative revelation of authentic divine being, and the unique and normative revelation of authentic human being.[19] In the miraculous, mysterious and profound event of the incarnation, life, death, resurrection and promised return of Jesus, there is disclosed the depth of the suffering love of God and the liberating love of God. There, also, is unveiled the height of sin and salvation. Thus, the measure of all things is Jesus Christ, "the objective reality and possibility of revelation" (Barth, 1956:1-44). Hence, the three sources of an authority of witness are fittingly distinguished as penultimate witnesses to, and as the means through which may be encountered, the ultimate witness of the revelation of God in Jesus Christ.[20] Understood in this way, Jesus Christ is God's bias. As "the objective reality and possibility of revelation," Jesus Christ is God's formal, material and functional bias. Jesus Christ is God's unique and normative model of revelation, mediated-manifested-authenticated in the unique and normative paradigm of and by the Holy Spirit.

In Relationship to a Concept of Jesus' Ministry

Consequently, the pattern of the church's internal and external life receives inspiration only as it subsists with a structure established by the person and work of Christ. The *Confession of 1967* describes such a pattern.[21]

> The life, death, resurrection, and promised coming of Jesus Christ has set the pattern for the church's mission. His life as a man involves the church in the common life of men. His service to men commits the church to work for every form of human well-being. His suffering makes the church sensitive to all the sufferings of mankind so that it sees the face of Christ in the faces of men in every kind of need. His crucifixion discloses to the church God's judgment on man's inhumanity to man and the awful consequences to its own complicity in injustice. In the power of the risen Christ and the hope of his coming the church sees the promise of God's renewal of man's life in society and of God's victory over all wrong.

> The church follows this pattern in the form of its life and in the method of its action. So to live and serve is to confess Christ as Lord. (Office of the General Assembly:9.32-9.33)

A denominational study paper, "The Nature and Practice of Ministry," also perceives the symbiotic structure of ministry.

> The basis and model for the Church and for ministry is to be found in Jesus Christ. The purpose of the Church as the people of God is to respond to God's revelation in Jesus Christ and by the power of the Holy Spirit to serve God's purpose in the world in continuity with what Jesus came to be and to do.

> As Jesus Christ was sent into the world for reconciliation so the Church is sent into the world. As Jesus Christ came to bear witness to the presence of transcendence, so the Church is steward of the mystery of the Kingdom. As Jesus Christ came to bring peace and justice, liberation and love, so the Church is to engage in the ministry of peace and justice, liberation and love. (Office of the Stated Clerk:4)

Therefore, the friendship model of ministry and its theology are patterned after the response to revelation that serves God and the world as a witness to the reconciliation of God in Jesus Christ.

The indissolvable connection of the Church's ministry with that of Christ's ministry is fundamental, according to John Macquarrie.

> The ministry of the Church is its service. Christ himself was identified with the "servant of the Lord" of whom we read in deutero-Isaiah. The Church, as continuing the work of Christ in the world, has also the role of a servant, and we can think of the image of the "servant of the Lord" as one that elucidates the character of the Church alongside the other images . . . such as "body of Christ" and "Israel of God."

> This linking of the ministry of the Church with the ministry of Christ is fundamental. All Christian ministry, whether we are thinking of the ministry of the whole people or of the ministry of those ordained to special offices, is a participation in the ministry of Christ. The many-sided character of Christian ministry is already foreshadowed in the many dimensions of Christ's ministry. He is the Servant, the Good Shepherd, the High Priest, the Prophet, and thus service, shepherding, priesthood, proclaiming are all constitutive elements of Christian ministry, though clearly the importance of each of these will vary in different forms of the ministry. (1977:420-421)

It is essential to connect the Church's ministry with Christ's ministry. Yet, in attempting to pattern human ministry after a pattern found in Jesus Christ, serious caution is fully sanctioned. Professor Shirley Guthrie preaches well the word in his sermon, "The Spirit and Witness: Listening to Luke 4:18-20."

> . . . If Jesus shares his Spirit with his followers, that does not mean that they become what he was or that they can or should try to do what he did. Christians are not little messiahs or saviors of the world. But those who live in the company of him who was and is the Messiah and Savior, and receive from him the same Spirit which he received, can expect some correspondence, similarities, between what being filled with the Spirit meant for him and what it means for them. They can expect in their own way to participate in the task the Spirit anointed him to fulfill, and they can expect also to share the consequences. (1978:36)

A non-blasphemous, friendly correspondence between the ministry of Christ and the model's ministry is negotiated.

Such negotiation is begun by seeing that the titles of Christ's office—prophet, priest, and king—can sparkle with new meaning through the office of friend. A friendly correspondence is officiated by Jurgen Moltmann in *The Church in the Power of the Spirit.*

> Jesus is only called "friend" in two passages in the New Testament. "The Son of man has come eating and drinking; and you say, 'Behold, a glutton and a drunkard, a friend of tax collectors and sinners!'" (Luke 7:34). These words are to be found in the discourse about John the Baptist. John neither ate bread nor drank wine, and was thought eccentric. Jesus accepted sinners, ate and drank with them, and was thought to disregard the law. This is the way the people described the obvious differences between Jesus and John the Baptist. The inner reason for Jesus' friendship with "tax collectors and sinners" was to be found in the joy of the messianic feast which he celebrated with them. It was not sympathy, it was overflowing joy in the kingdom of God, a joy that sought to share and to welcome, that drew him to people who were outcasts in the eyes of the law . . .

> According to John 15:13f., Jesus declares himself the friend of his disciples and calls them into the new life of friendship. "Greater love has no man than this, that a man lay down his life for his friends. You are my friends if you do what I command you." Here the sacrifice of a [person's] own life for . . . friends is the highest form of love. Whereas love in general can be interpreted as "existence for the other, pure and simple," friendship leads to actually risking one's life to protect a friend. When John makes friendship the motive for Christ's suffering and death, then he means by this love clear-sighted faithfulness and conscious self-devotion for the salvation of others. Through the death of their friend the disciples become his friends forever. On their side they remain in the circle of his friendship when they keep his commandments and become friends of one another. According to John too Jesus' friendship with the disciples springs from joy: "These things I have spoken to you, that my joy may be in you, and that your joy may be full" (15:11). That is the divine joy, the joy of eternal life, the overflowing joy that confers fellowship and gives joy to others. He has come, he suffers and dies for them out of the divine joy, not out of condescension, and for the joy of those who are his, not out of sympathy. That is why the disciples are called "friends" and not "servants" (15:15). (1977:116-118)

Jesus is a friend of sinners. Although our friendship can never equal his friendship, still it is possible to picture at least our being a human friend with humankind. Yet, Jesus is also a friend of God. How can it be postulated reasonably and respectfully that human beings can be friends of and with God? Again, Moltmann makes a cogent contribution in *The Trinity and the Kingdom* that spans a panoramic view of this reality and possibility. Rather than thinking in terms of any historical development, the author articulates three levels in the dimension of freedom. The view is wonderful in meaning and beauty as "Freedom in the Kingdom of the Triune God" (1981:219-222). Here it is sufficient merely to mention the triadic dimension of freedom that is pronounced in the trinitarian history of God with humankind. (1) In the kingdom of the Father, women and men live in the freedom of servants of the Lord. (2) In the kingdom of the Son, women and men live in the freedom of children of the Father. (3) In the kingdom of the Spirit, the servants of the Lord and the children of the Father now become, and live in the freedom of, God's friends (1981:219-222). Moltmann makes an intriguing, almost mystical elixir. He starts with a concept of Kant, pours in the correlation of the divine-human encounter and mixes it all up with a phrase of Hegel.

> . . . Kant said that friendship combines affection with respect. God makes men and women . . . friends [of God] by inclining affection-ately towards them and by listening to them. [God] makes people . . . friends [of God] by letting them find themselves and by respecting their responsibility. People draw near to God by praying without beg-ging and by talking to [God] in a way that shows they respect [God's] liberty. The prayer of the friend is neither the servility of the servant nor the importunity of the child; it is a conversation in the freedom of love, that shares and allows the other to share. Friendship is "the con-crete concept of freedom." (1981:221)

The concept of human beings as friends of God circumscribes an encounter, a divine and human friendship encounter. It is an encounter between two subjects in which human subjectivity is completely honored while maintaining that God remains always the most powerful and al-ways takes the initiative. God's awesome friendship is neither brutal nor arbitrary. Yet, there can be a kind of rigid theological formulation that serves only to stifle the inter-subjective encounter. However, the ele-ments of surprise and unpredictability can be preserved along with con-serving the greater power of God, human responsibility and the reliable promise of the means of grace. The latter three variables do not need to be structured into a forced plot which pushes the encounter down a developmental path. Rather, the freedom of God's encountering can be acclaimed. The friendship encounter sustains and nourishes freedom in every direction.[22]

A necessary warning needs to be given about the divine-human friendship encounter. God's friendship action is not always safe and easy. It is also dangerous and difficult. The divine-human friendship encounter does produce genuine hope. It also produces genuine crisis. Such inspired hope and crisis together are a process of renewal. Berkhof flags the constituent moments in this renewal process around three tracks: "condemnation-justification-sanctification, repentance-faith-freedom-love, or despair-relaxation-effort" (1986:471).

The process of renewal as conveyed through the model's overarching object (aim) is the ever-increasing qualitative and quantitive freedom of God's friendship. It sounds so soothing and civil. Yet, the social, economic and political increase of God's friendship freedom let loose in the world by the invasion of the Holy Spirit may be provocative and subversive. The vertical dimension of the divine-human friendship encounter can likewise be disturbing while it maintains freedom. The divine-human friendship encounter creates struggle and progress.

> Struggle and progress apparently do not exclude but include each other. The progress happens amid the struggle, and apparently the struggle does not lead to stagnation, but to steady progress. The question arises, how are we to conceive of this progress in this conflict situation? In our opinion, we are to look in four directions. (1) Only in the brokenness of the conflict does the believer really get to know himself [and herself] in his [and her] opposition against God; so long as that opposition remains unchallenged, it may seem to lie dormant and can easily be underestimated; the struggle is thus an advancing in self-knowledge. (2) Consequently the struggle also implies progress in living from the acquittal; the better we get to know ourselves, the less we expect from ourselves, and the more we fall back on God's grace as the decisive foundation of our life. (3) But precisely this growing relaxation inspires to fresh and greater efforts, making the struggle more intense. (4) And coupled with that, the conflict spreads to more and more areas of our life; for all the time we discover new areas of conduct and thought which so far were not yet involved in the process of renewal and where new opportunities await us, for example, in the use of our charismata for the upbuilding of the church, in respect to our

political insights, in fresh conciliatory approaches to our enemies, in changes in how we spend our income, in the struggle against discriminatory practices and situations. (Berkhof, 1986:475)

The situation seems to be that on both sides of the divine-human friendship encounter, in addition to struggle and progress, there is defeat. In order to avoid the wistful expectation of and the myoptic reporting of uninterrupted safety, ease and progress regarding the work of God's friendship freedom, it is prudent for the theme of defeat to be sounded and to be soundly remembered.

To a great extent official church history is the story of the defeats of the Spirit. But [the Spirit] does not stop from venturing onto this battlefield. Continually [the Spirit] stirs people and groups, mostly minorities, into action, so that in witness and service they may do that which the church owes to the world. These get to experience to the full what it means to suffer in the world, but mostly they are made to suffer even more from ecclesiastical institutions and majorities—until a following generation erects monuments in honor of the prophets who had been stoned by their [parents].

What God has in mind with the church is still far from realized. We are no further than a small beginning. But the struggle continues, and the participants know that what is at issue here is the meaning of all of existence and, furthermore, that the continuance of this struggle is a sign of the victory which the Spirit will some day achieve over our recalcitrance. Therefore the church is the place where we are constantly being compelled to step ahead ourselves, and where we learn to want more than the present state of affairs and what has so far been achieved. Precisely on account of all the disobedience and failure that surrounds this calling, by being this battlefield the church is the experimental garden and first-fruits her Lord had in mind. For in order to get this battle going this new community was called into existence. (Berkhof, 1986:426)

The existence of the first-fruits of this communal friendship encounter can be seen in the light of ministry through James Wharton's provocative essay, "Theology and Ministry in Hebrew Scriptures," which analyzes ministry in the Old Testament. God's ministry with humankind is revealed in terms of God's "freedom from and for" humankind, and humankind's ministry to God is revealed in terms of humankind's "free-

dom from and for" God (1981:36). Another fruit of this friendship encounter is that humankind experiences "freedom from and for" each
other. Wharton's work is full of wisdom. Its insight is gratefully received throughout the model and its theology.

The model exalts Jesus as the perfect friend who is perfectly free
from and for God and humankind. The freedom of this friendship takes
the form of witness. Jesus is not only a friend, but a friend who is a
witness. Jesus is the friend of sinners on behalf of God, and the friend of
God on behalf of sinners. Jesus is the living witness to the revelation of
the reality and possibility of God's friendship with humankind,
humankind's friendship with God, and humankind's friendship with humankind.

Furthermore, the model features Jesus as a friend who is a witness
who bids us to be the same.[23] Shirley Guthrie teaches convincingly the
solid, scriptural conduct of witness through his book *Diversity in Faith—
Unity in Christ*.

> According to Acts 1:8, the very last word of the risen Jesus to his
> disciples was the command to be his witnesses, beginning where they
> were "and to the end of the earth". This command announces the main
> theme of the whole book. Throughout Acts the primary task of Chris-
> tians is to bear witness to the story of the life, the death, and especially
> the resurrection of Jesus and to the consequences of these events for
> Christian faith and life. The title "witness" itself is not often applied to
> Christians in the rest of the New Testament (though according to the
> first chapter of John's Gospel, John the Baptist the first Christian,
> identified himself as a witness, and in John 15:27 Jesus tells his dis-
> ciples that they are to be his witnesses). But it is clear that "witness" is
> what all the first Christians, including the writers of the Gospels and
> the letters, understood themselves to be and what they invited hearers
> of the gospel to become: witnesses in attitude, word, and action to
> what God has done, is doing, and promises to do in the crucified and
> risen Jesus of Nazareth, the living and coming Lord and Savior.
>
> The definition of Christians as witnesses thus meets one of the main
> requirements . . . for an adequate understanding of what it means to be
> a Christian: it is biblically based and it is broad enough to incorporate
> not just a part but the whole of what is called precisely the New Testa-
> ment "witness" to Jesus. Moreover, this fundamental biblical under-
> standing of what it means to be a Christian preserves the strengths and
> corrects the weaknesses of orthodox, liberal, and pietistic Christianity.
> (1986:83-84)

Thus, Christians are friends who witness to Jesus Christ, who witnesses to God's friendship. The unequivocal, sanctifying quality of God's friendship can be characterized by procuring five famous categories of H. Richard Niebuhr: it is not friendship "against culture," not friendship "of culture," not friendship "above culture," not friendship "and culture in paradox," but friendship "transforming culture" (1951). Christ is the transformer, the living example and provider of friendship with God and humankind. Christ transforms culture as a witness to God's transforming friendship, and Christians transform culture, however modestly, as a witness to Christ's transforming friendship, which of course in turn witnesses to God's friendship.

The model continues to research a pattern of ministry in Christ. Jesus, as a friend who witnesses to God's friendship, incarnates friendship in a community. Jesus lives in community a truly human life of friendship.

Jesus lived a truly human life.

> Jesus was what we are. He grew up in a family and a society troubled by the common problems of the world. His knowledge was limited by his time and place in history. He felt deeply the joy of friendship and the hurt of being rejected. Jesus prayed, struggled with temptation, knew anger, and was subject to suffering and death. He was like us in every way except sin.

> Jesus was what we should be. He served his Father with complete trust and unwavering obedience. He loved all kinds of people and accepted their love. In constant dependence upon the Holy Spirit, Jesus allowed no temptation or threat to keep him from loving God with his whole being and his neighbor as himself.

> We recognize in Jesus what God created us to be. He exposes our failure to live as he lived. He demonstrates the humanity God promises to give us through him. (Presbyterian Publishing House:163)

Likewise, we are beckoned to be friends who witness to God's friendship in community. The dynamics of this type of community are described by authors Joseph Hough and John Cobb in *Christian Identity and Theological Education*.

> The character of the church as a human community means that members of the church are bound together in ways that transcend their own

autonomy. As in other human communities, they are united with one another without violating their individuality. As Paul Tillich has shown, the relationship between individuality and participation in community is such that one can become a true individual only through participation, and one can authentically participate only as one's individuality is given expression in the community. When a human community embraces these polarities in balance, it can be said to be a humanizing community. (50)

Moltmann also addresses these polarities and does so in a novel way:

. . . Socialization and individuation are two sides of one and the same operation in the history of the Spirit. The Spirit leads men and women into the fellowship of the messianic people, at the same time giving everyone his [and her] own place and his [and her] particular charge. In messianic history everyone finds his [and her] new identity in Christ and the place to which he [and she] personally [belong]. By socializing, the Spirit individualizes; and by individualizing, [the Spirit] socializes. (1977:306)

Jesus is a friend who witnesses to God's friendship in a community. The experience of God's friendship in a Christian community is the experience of *koinonia*. Jesus is a friend who witnesses to God's friendship in a friendship community of *koinonia*. In his book, *The Church*, Wallace Alston paints colorfully the kinship of *koinonia*.

Jesus Christ was no longer physically present with the early Christian church. Nevertheless, the first Christians had a sense of his real presence in their midst through the presence of the Holy Spirit. The word often used in the New Testament to describe this sense of presence which bound men and women together in common faith and life is "koinonia." The word is a transliteration of a Greek word for which no English word is an adequate translation. Koinonia is often translated "fellowship" or "community," but neither is adequate to carry the intended meaning. In the New Testament, koinomia is used for the intimate relationship that Christians have with God (I John 1:3), with Jesus Christ (I John 1:3; Phil. 3:10), with the Spirit (Phil. 2:1), with the mystery of God's plan hidden for ages (Eph. 3:9), with the gospel (Phil. 1:5), with the mission of the church (II Cor. 8:4), and with others in the church (Acts 2:42; I John 1:3). The word points to the fact that those upon whom the Holy Spirit descended at Pentecost were drawn into a common life and ministry by a common gospel, rooted and grounded in a common relationship to God, Father, Son, and Holy Spirit. They entered into this koinonia by repentance and baptism to evidence that this association was something brand new. The Christian koinonia had continuity with the past. The first Christians claimed the history of Israel as their heritage. But they nevertheless were convinced that Christian community represented a new act of God in accordance with the promise of the risen Christ and in fulfillment of ancient prophecy. Paul Lehmann . . . described the koinonia as "the fellowship-creating reality of Christ's presence in the world."

. . . It was in the Christian koinonia that men and women participated in a close and personal relationship with God. It was in the Christian koinonia that these same men and women were most likely to be understood, accepted, respected, and befriended. Here Christian men and women came to the deepest and freest self-realization, not through self-analysis but in the exchange of life and mutual service. Here they experienced God's renovating activity in the world. (34-36)

Alston correctly pictures *koinonia* with its vast and priceless importance. Yet, it is even more abundantly more than fellowship. It is a mysterious extravaganza. The model terms *koinonia* as the friendship-creating reality of Christ's transforming presence in the world. Jesus is the revelation of the objective reality and possibility of God's friendship with humankind, the revelation of the objective reality and possibility of humankind's friendship with God, and the revelation of the objective reality and possibility of humankind's friendship with humankind, which is *koinonia,* which is nothing less than an expression of the kingdom of God active in the world.

We also are called to be friends who witness to God's friendship kingdom of *koinonia.* However, not only are individuals called to be friends who witness to God's friendship in a friendship community of *koinonia,* the entire *koinonia* community is called to live in *koinonia* and called to witness to the *koinonia* of God. All communal members, ordained and non-ordained, are summoned to the ministry as friends who witness to God's *koinonia* with humankind. The entire friendship community exists for the purpose of friendship with the entire global community. The church, as the *koinonia* community, exists for the purpose of transforming the world into a globe of *koinonia* friendship. Understandably, the church as the *koinonia* community of God takes the form of "a fellowship of friends" (Moltmann, 1977:314): friends who live in the *koinonia* friendship of God and, therefore, friends who witness to Jesus Christ, who is the revelation of God's *koinonia* friendship with human-kind.

The model still explores a pattern of ministry in Christ. Jesus is a friend who witnesses to God's friendship with humankind. The content of this witnessing activity is suffering love and liberating love.[24] Jesus manifests friendship with God on behalf of humankind, and manifests friendship with humankind on behalf of God, through the task of his friendship of suffering and liberating love. We continue to listen to Guthrie's sermon as he witnesses to Christ's anointed task according to Luke 4:18-20. It is the task of radical friendship.[25]

> What were the consequences for [Jesus] when he set out to fulfill that task? Being filled with the Holy Spirit and thus becoming a "spiritual" person meant friendship with prostitutes, dishonest business men, po-litical revolutionaries, religious heretics, social outcasts. It meant of-fending the moral and religious leaders of society. It got him into trouble with the government for disturbing the peace and upsetting law and order. And finally, being a spiritual person filled with the Holy Spirit meant being arrested, tried in court, sentenced to capital punish-ment, and executed as a common criminal. (1978:36)

Serious attention to the suffering and liberating friendship of Christ for the sake of God and humankind has the power to exorcise one of any lingering cultural connotations of sentimentality that still may be hover-ing around the concept of friend.

Jesus' friends in the New Testament are not sentimentalists. Many of them are historical eye-witnesses to "the objective reality and possibility of revelation." Berkhof recounts this primal history.

> *The historical dimension.* God's mighty acts are acts in history. They can only be transmitted and made credible to the coming generations by the juridically valid testimony of real eye-witnesses. So the martus in the New Testament is, if not exclusively so at any rate mainly, the eye-witness. "The Spirit will bear witness to me; and you also are witnesses, because you have been with me from the beginning" (John 15.26f.). Jesus did not call all his adherents to follow him. He elected a small group to be eye-witnesses in order to become the fundamental witnesses to the world. No one can be an apostle who was not a dis-ciple before. So the eye-witnesses, the *martures* in the strict juridical and historical sense of the word, form a very limited group. Some

doubted whether Paul could be regarded as one of them. His answer was: "Am I not an apostle? Have I not seen Jesus our Lord?" (I Cor. 9.1). The original witness can say: "Which we have heard, which we have seen with our eyes, which we have looked upon and touched with our hands, concerning the word of life—we testify to it and proclaim also to you" (I John 1.1-3). And in Acts 10.40f.: "God raised Jesus on the third day and made him manifest, not to all the people but to us who were chosen by God as witnesses, who ate and drank with him after he rose from the dead." It is clear that in the New Testament the main object of that witness is the resurrection as the revelation of Jesus' divine calling and the dawning of the new creation. Witness in the biblical sense is not conceivable without having the resurrection in the centre. Without that, Christian witness would be distorted (as has often been the case) into a communication of general religious convictions. (1964:101-102)

This primal history of witness contains two essential paradigmatic expressions of God's friendship with humankind.

The most profound revelation of God's friendship of suffering love is the crucifixion of Christ (Moltmann, 1974). Christ suffers ultimate forsakenness by God for the sake of friendship love for God and humankind. Although our depth of pain can never experience the unfathomable abyss of Christ's grieving cry of dereliction, we are commissioned as friends to witness to God's friendship of suffering love with humankind. Such suffering is bounded only by the limits of friendship and may involve a rueful death.

The most profound revelation of God's friendship of liberating love is the resurrection of Christ (Moltmann, 1967). Although our joy does not shout from personally experiencing the miracle of the resurrection, we are commissioned as friends to witness to God's friendship of liberating love with humankind. Such liberating is bounded only by the limits of friendship and may also involve a rueful death.

Some of Jesus' friends in the New Testament are eye-witnesses, but they are more than eye-witnesses. Subsequent historical and contemporary friends of Jesus are not eye-witnesses, but they are more than eye-witnesses. Berkhof describes the quality that is more than being eye-witnesses.

The existential dimension. . . . In emphasizing only the juridical, historical and institutional aspects of the apostolic witness, we are in danger of forgetting that the eye-witnesses were more than just reporters.

They testified to Jesus as the Son of God, the Saviour and the Conqueror. So they testified to a reality which their bodily eyes as such could see no more than the eyes of their many contemporaries who did not believe in Jesus. They saw Jesus as the Christ with eyes of faith, granted by the Holy Spirit. Moreover, they surrendered their lives to the New Lord; and their witness to those outside was for that reason not a mere communication but an appeal to conversion. By their witness they wanted to awake in succeeding generations the same faith, surrender and witness: "That which we have seen and heard we proclaim also to you, so that you may have fellowship with us" (I John 1.3). "He who believes in the Son of God has the testimony in himself" (I John 5.10). That is the reason why even in the New Testament the word "witness" is not limited to the eye-witnesses. In the Revelation, the word *martus is* used for what we call "a martyr" (2.13; 11.3; 17.6), a [person] who pays the price of his [or her] existence for his [or her] witness. In Acts 22.20, Stephen also is called a "witness" in connection with his death. He is not a witness, however, because he is killed, rather he is killed because he is a witness. Our use of the word "martyr" is an undue narrowing of the sense of the word. Nevertheless, this usage reminds us rightly of the existential nature of all witness.

In this existential character there is no difference between the eyewitnesses and the later generations. The apostles are not the exclusive witnesses. They lead the way and we follow them. We are dependent on them. In faith and confession there is, however, no difference: "Blessed are those who have not seen and yet believe" (John 20.29).

In our days some are inclined to put witnessing by words over against witnessing by existence. The New Testament does not give the slightest reason for such an opposition. On the contrary, in the New Testament the witnesses always pay with their existence for their words. No testimony is a real Christian testimony if the verbal proclamation of the resurrected Jesus is not presupposed in one way or another. No testimony is a real Christian testimony either, if this faith in the resurrected Jesus does not occupy and direct the whole witnessing person. We are no mere reporters but signs of the resurrection. (1964:103-104)

"We are no mere reporters" of the crucifixion and the resurrection: we are witnessing signs of the crucifixion and the resurrection. Signs of the crucifixion and the resurrection can be given socially, economically and politically. Again, Shirley Guthrie extends indispensable assistance through the book *Diversity in Faith—Unity in Christ*. Three categories are provided for the extension of a witness to Jesus Christ and a witness to God's suffering-liberating presence in the world. The categories are "poor oppressed creatures," "poor oppressed sinners," and "the politically and economically poor and oppressed" (1986:92-104). Both Jesus and human beings are friends who witness to God's friendship of suffering-liberating love for humankind.

The model sculptures the witnessing clay in this way: out of gratitude to God who befriends, who gives the gift of God's friendship, the gift of *koinonia,* the gift of the suffering-liberating knowledge and presence of God in a community of friends—the *koinonia* community follows Jesus Christ, the witness to God's friendship of suffering-liberating love, by being witnessing friends who suffer with and liberate friends for the purpose of friendship with God and humankind.

The model moves forward to find more ministerial ground in a pattern of Christ. An active imagination and a serious reading of the gospels can uncover some substantiation in the life and ministry of Jesus for the model's ministerial functions and its disciplined practices. In some ways, Jesus is a preacher-worship leader friend, a visitor-counselor friend, a teacher friend, a missionary friend, and an administrator friend. Only in the sense of maybe being in a rabbinical tradition can Jesus approach being anything like a judicatory friend and a professional friend.

Victor Furnish, in his monograph "Theology and Ministry in the Pauline Letters," documents that Paul is a bountiful embodiment of ministerial functions and communal disciplined practices. Paul is a preacher who proclaims the gospel, an apostle who builds communities of faith and a teacher who nurtures communities of faith (106-120). The whole of Paul's ministry grows in grateful devotion to the personal commission of the risen Christ, who is thereby through Paul ministering to the community of Christ. Jesus, as Lord of the Church, appears to authorize and bless the substance and form of Paul's ministry. Thus, the ministerial functions and the communal disciplined practices can be considered to be in continuity with Christ's identity and ministry, as they witness to the person and work of Christ.

This brief allusion to Paul leads to an institutional facet of witness, which is presented by Berkhof.

The institutional dimension. This is another consequence of the historical character of Christian witnessing. Jesus chose twelve witnesses.

This number was not accidental. It had to do with the structure of
Israel with its twelve tribes. This Israel has now to be transformed into
a new Israel which can be the witness of its King towards the nations.
The apostolic twelve have to function as the bones of this renewed
Israel. God continued in the manner of his historic work. When Judas
fails, a successor has to be chosen, of course (as Peter formulates it):
"One of the men who accompanied us during all the time that the Lord
Jesus went in and out among us" (Acts 1.21). The calling of Paul, one
"untimely born" who nevertheless "worked harder than any of them,"
provides that God is not bound to . . . institutional forms. Nevertheless
Paul sets high value on his being acknowledged by the twelve, because
there is but one testimony and God is not a God of confusion but of
peace. When the apostles died, the institutional form of the twelve
died also. Now their testimony, varied and yet one, is embodied in the
canon of the New Testament. That is the testimony of the eye-witnesses which is still present among us and on which our witness depends. Therefore our witness has authority in so far as it is connected
with the apostolic witness and functions within the apostolic Church,
the communion which stands in the succession of the apostolic testimony. (1964:102-103)

A contemporary testimony that videos the ministerial functions and
the communal disciplined practices in sound witnessing obedience to the
continuing ministry of Christ records in technicolor and stereo the high-
fidelity church as a worshipping, humanizing, integrating, caring, evan-
gelistic, repentant and holy community of friends who live for the poor,
for women, for all people and for the world (Hough and Cobb:47-76).

The communal disciplined practices are the grist in the theological
mill. The communal disciplined practices are the intermingled matrix
containing the sources of an authority of witness in scripture, in tradition
and in personal experience, as well as containing the means used to approximate an historical norm, an experiential norm and a semblance of a
systematic norm. The communal disciplined practices are the tools of the
theological trade and their communal practice is the contextual setting in
which theological irresponsibility in theory and *praxis* is minimized.

In a call to ethical responsibility, Donald Browning, in *Religious
Ethics and Pastoral Care*, offers an extremely helpful hermeneutical model
which can assist in guiding the church toward a general moral consensus
(53-71). The dialogical model is itself a crystallization of several com-

munal disciplined practices in action. Although the model specifically confronts ethical concerns, its use need not be limited to morality or to pastoral care. The model is quite encompassing. According to Browning's model, moral diagnosis arbitrates its progressive dialogue through five paths of an objective arena, and through five paths of a subjective arena. The objective perspective levels are "metaphorical," "obligational," "tendency-need," "contextual-predictive," and "rule-role." The subjective ["Characterological (Aretaic)"] levels are "Faith Development," "Moral Development," "Emotional-Motivational Development," "Ego Development (Reality Perception)," and "Rule-Role Development" (57). Browning's model can enable the church to become not only "a community of moral discourse" (120-122), but also a community of social, economic and political discourse, which is also a way of being a community of theological discourse. The forensic model is an incisive way of summoning the church to and engaging the church in its communal disciplined practice of being open to and critical of itself and society. Its potential is pastorally prophetic.[26]

The communal disciplined practices are the concrete, disciplined manifestations of friends who have been befriended by God. Out of gratitude to God for God's befriending action, these friends become practical communal theologians who witness, in and with a fellowship of friends, to God's *koinonia* in Christ, God's friendship of suffering-liberating love for and with humankind, which is also God's action of reconciliation.

The over-arching aim of the model is the freedom of God's friendship.[27] Freedom means the ever-expanding qualitative and quantitative increase of God's friendship. The places where this friendship freedom rings are similar to the places where Jesus reigns in loving friendship freedom: synagogue/church, home, community and world.

In this world, the life of Christian faith is "existence in the execution of this task" of witness, according to Karl Barth (1962:573-574). The edict to execute such a comprehensive vocational task can seem to be a heavy yoke of activism. The concept of this task of witness, in claiming to be supreme, can also be interpreted as being one-sided. Shortly after the first appearance in English of the volume in which Barth announces this declaration, Berkhof shares a profound message, and in so doing addresses both of these criticisms. The Dutch professor of Leiden delivers to a meeting in Mexico of the World Council of Churches a creative critique at the end of his study of the biblical concept of "Witnesses."

Finality. This is the word I use to express a last feature of Christian witness, the fact that witness is not an appendix to Christian life, nor even a part of this life, but the very meaning of this life. Or should I say one of the meanings of the Christian life? To be frank, I am hesitant on this point. Let me first describe what I have in mind. Karl Barth has in the latest volume of his *Church Dogmatics* developed a theology of witness on the basis of Christ's prophetic office. One of the most excellent and exciting parts of this rich book is that about "The Christian as a witness"[1] Here Barth argues that witness and witness alone is the essence, the aim and the common denominator of Christian life. Until now, personal salvation has been regarded as having this final significance. Barth attacks that age-old conviction. He points to the fact that the Bible does not know stories of conversion but of calling, in which the personal element plays but a secondary role. If personal salvation were the aim of our calling, Barth demonstrates, then Christ would become a means to that end and the Christian would become a mere consumer. Even more, in this way Christianity would become an egotistic enterprise. Let me quote only one forceful passage: "Can the community of Jesus Christ . . . really be only, or at any rate essentially and decisively, a kind of institution of salvation, the foremost and comprehensive means of salvation, as Calvin self-evidently assumed and said? Is not every form of egocentricity excused, and even confirmed and sanctified, if egocentricity in this sacred form is the divinely willed meaning of Christian existence, and the Christian song of praise consists finally only in a many-tongued but monotonous 'For me, for me!' and similar possessive expressions."[2] This conception of Barth's has tremendous consequences for our ecclesiastical, missionary and personal life. It is a very welcome reaction against an egotistic individualism which for centuries has corrupted our understanding of the Christian faith. I wonder, however, whether Barth is not in danger of expelling one kind of one-sidedness by introducing another. I have two reasons for thinking so. First, the unmistakable and strong emphasis in the New Testament on personal salvation for its own sake. Second, the consideration that witness in itself cannot be final, because it is always a means to an end, i.e., to salvation (taking the word in its broadest sense, including future and present, soul and body, the relation to God and that to the neighbour). Salvation presupposes witness; witness presupposes salvation. They are mutually the means and the end of one another. For that reason the character of finality cannot be ascribed either to witness or to salvation. It belongs to a reality of which both are the two interrelated aspects. Can we give a name to that reality? Barth himself offers the right name, though he identifies it with witness. The name is: participation. That is the final meaning of our Christian existence—to become participants in the Kingdom of God, in its blessings and in its tasks. In that Kingdom, we are neither mere consumers nor mere labourers. We consume in order to work; and we work in order that others may consume. Both are one: saved to save! We witness in our saved existences. The acme of our salvation is the fulfillment of the promise: "Ye shall be my witnesses." (1964:104-106)[28]

The friendship model of ministry as a normative theological mediating structure embraces the critical theological analysis and synthesis of both Berkhof and Barth by saying that participation in the kingdom of God takes the form of witness, and therefore, witness is predicated upon participation. Witness is the *a posteriori* and participation is the *a priori.* The model's theology agrees with Barth: existence in this life is the execution of the task of witness. The model's theology also agrees with Berkhof: "[P]articipation . . . is the final meaning of our Christian existence—to become participants in the Kingdom of God, in its blessings and in its tasks" (1964:106). Existence (that is, participation) in this life (that is, in this life's experience of the kingdom of God) takes the comprehensive form of witness. A more direct statement declares that Christian existence equals witnessing participation in the kingdom of God.[29]

This kind of participation, a receiving and a giving, is the book's initial concept of ministry.

> . . . The operative understanding is that ministry is both a gift and a task from God, in which there is a receiving and a giving in response to divine grace.[30]

This kind of participation is, furthermore, the ministerial model's object (aim), which is the freedom of God's friendship, which means participation in the freedom of God's friendship. Participation in the freedom of God's friendship, the kingdom of God, takes the form of witness, which is participation in the ministry of friendship. Witnessing participation in the kingdom of God is, then, the process of receiving and giving the witness of God's friendship of suffering and liberating love, all in response to grace.

Another way to envision this comprehensive unitive task of witness as not being a heavy, one-sided yoke is to speculate that the model's charge to us to be friends who witness to Jesus Christ is not right because we are commanded by anyone or even commanded by scripture so to be and to do. Rather, we are commanded to be friends who witness to Jesus Christ because it is right. It is right because it reveals humankind's true nature. Persons are called to be friends who witness to Jesus Christ because in fulfilling that task they discover who they are. We are called to live-out our true calling, to be our true selves.[31] Participating in the task of witness is our calling, our vocation, our ministry.

Therefore, the model proposes that the church's identity and its ministry can be vibrantly empathic with the identity and the ministry of Jesus, at least in the limited sense of the earlier said subscription to a friendly correspondence between the two. Also, the model proposes that the church's identity and its ministry are identical: being friends who witness to Jesus Christ, the revelation of God's friendship of suffering-liberating love with humankind. Modeled here is a way of integrated being which issues forth in a way of integrated doing. True ministry encourages persons to discover who they are truly created, sustained, governed, judged, reconciled and redeemed to be in *a koinonia* friendship community of friends.

The idea of witness is, indeed, quite broad. Its comprehensiveness includes Barth's assertion that the threefold nature of the Church's ministry is proclaiming, explaining and applying the gospel (1962:843-854). The comprehensiveness of the idea of witness also includes Berkhof's serious and superb pointing to the expansive dimensions of the biblical concept of witness. A review recalls Berkhof's previously cited dimensions of witness: "the trinitarian dimension," "the juridical dimension," "the cosmic dimension," "the historical dimension," "the existential dimension," "the institutional dimension," and the dimension of "finality" (1962:98-106). Strengthened by the dimensional implications drawn thus far, the construct of witness can emerge as grand. Yet, persons who witness are delivered from warped grandiosity. Here we see Berkhof witness again.

> *The indicative character of Christian witness.* Closely related to its historical character is the way in which it directs attention beyond itself. This feature is also very prominent in the Gospel of John, particularly in the person of John the Baptist. The witness is not sent to make himself [or herself] interesting and to express his [or her] personal convictions, sentiments and experiences. . . . [One's] whole work and existence is a finger pointing to . . . [the] crucified and risen Saviour: "He was not the light, but came to bear witness to the light" (1.8). "He confessed, he did not deny but confessed: 'I am not the

Christ' . . . 'I am the voice'" (1.20-23).   He said: "Behold the Lamb
of God!" (1.36). "The friend of the bridegroom, who stands and hears
him, rejoices greatly at the bridegroom's voice . . . he must increase
but I must decrease" (3.29f). Every witness stands under this law.
[Every witness] points away from . . . [oneself], and in so far as . . .
[the witness] speaks about himself [or herself] in . . . relation to . . .
[the] Lord, it is not to make himself [or herself] but to make . . . [the]
Lord more important to . . . [the] hearers: "For it is not ourselves that
we proclaim; we proclaim Christ Jesus as Lord, and ourselves as your
servants, for Jesus' sake" (II Cor. 4.5). (1964:102)

"The indicative character of Christian witness" continues to be heard.
The conclusion to professor Guthrie's sermon, "The Spirit and Witness,"
clinches the limitation of and claims the biblical promise of witness.

. . . [T]he same Jesus, the same Lukan Jesus, who said at the beginning of his ministry on his way to the cross, "The Spirit of the Lord is
upon me," also said at the end of his ministry after his resurrection,
"You shall receive power when Holy Spirit has come upon you, and
you shall be my witness . . . to the end of the earth."

When the Holy Spirit has come upon you, you shall be my witnesses—
witnesses to Christ. Thank God we don't have to get involved in the
disastrous enterprise of bearing witness to ourselves or to the church,
and what the Spirit has done for us and given to us, and how great we
are. We can be witnesses to the one who, filled with the Spirit, really
is at work bringing about the justice of the kingdom of God in the
world.

Only witnesses. Not substitutes for him who are empowered to do
what he does, or who have the terrible burden of having to do what he
does. Just witnesses, invited to the modest task of participating in the
mission he began long before we ever came along, the mission he even
now is fulfilling and will complete with or without our feeble, blunder-
ing efforts to help. Witnesses who therefore can throw ourselves into
the battle with confidence and hope just because its outcome does not
depend on us.

You shall receive power—not just power to become impressive religious personalities, but something much greater than that—power to
be and do and say what is necessary to fulfill the task the Spirit gives
us to fulfill. For at the same time the Spirit gives us our mission, [the

Spirit] also promises the ability to fulfill it. [The Spirit] gives what [the Spirit] demands. We can count on it. (1978:40)

In Relationship to a Concept of Change

Given that the witness of the model may be able to find some footing in the pattern of a concept of Jesus' ministry, it remains to be seen how the model may conceptualize change.

God constitutes the human community in such an order that it is objectively and subjectively oriented for the freedom of ever-expanding and enriching theocentric communal friendship with God and humankind. Out of its finite yet real friendship freedom, humankind objectively and subjectively disorients itself by exhibiting a strong abortive addiction (May, 1988) to self-atrophying, idiosyncratic associations within egocentric enclaves, megastructures and mediating structures. The constrictive egocentric preference is both the progeny of and also further begets rebellion against God (active and passive), enmity between humans and other creatures, fraction and distortion of a naturally good creation, self-destruction and planetary exploitation.

This egocentric addiction is a human fault. In his *Ethics from a Theocentric Perspective*, James Gustafson produces a precise and indicting documentary on the matter of human fault. It is not possible or necessary to replay fully his taping of the entire faulty human drama. It is satisfactory first to hear the theme established in a general introduction.

> . . . There is idolatry; from early biblical writings forward the term persists. It refers to absolute confidence in objects, realities, and persons that do not merit that confidence. It refers to the surrender of accountability for oneself by in effect enslaving oneself to some person or cause. It refers to too much confidence in appropriate "objects," that do not bear the excessive trust we have in them. There is pride; we know about it not only from the biblical religions but also from the Greek literary and moral traditions. It is that overweening trust in the rectitude of our judgments, the superiority of our perspectives, that keeps us from due self-criticism and from hearing the criticisms of others. There is infidelity. It refers to the breaking of bonds in which duties and obligations are formed, to our capacities for betrayal of persons and deception of them, to our resort to expedience to justify our failures to act when our moral obligations clearly demand our defense of those human values to which we profess loyalty. There

is sloth. It is not only laziness per se, but also complacency, diffuseness, irresponsibility, and lack of effort to discipline ourselves. . . . These roots of improper actions are, in a theological account, seen to be grounded in part in being improperly related to God, and to other things in relation to God. (192)

The egocentric fault is essentially a relational fault, a friendship fault, a faulty friendship. Next, we listen to Gustafson's theme and variation.

There are four facets of the "human fault" that are experienced, I dare to affirm, by all human beings. The Christian tradition has had insight into all four: the experience of misplaced trust or confidence (the traditional problem of "idolatry"), the experience of misplaced valuations of objects of desire (the traditional problem of wrongly ordered love), the experience of erroneous perceptions of the relations of things to each other and our understanding of things (the traditional problem of "corrupt" rationality), and the experience of unfulfilled obligations and duties (the traditional problem of disobedience). The doctrines of sin in the theological tradition arise out of these experiences; what makes them "sin" is that persons have a measure of accountability to God in each. Each involves a disordering of proper human relationships to other persons and to the world around us and each involves a somewhat disordered relation to the powers that sustain life and bear down upon it. The four are frequently interrelated with each other both in the sorts of agents we are (thus references to "sinful human nature") and the sorts of actions we engage in (thus references to "sinful acts"). All four are "inevitable." (294)

How and why the quadruple fault is inevitable is not self-evident. Macquarrie gives a plausible speculation in his *An Existentialist Theoloqy: A Comparison of Heidegger and Bultmann.*

. . . [H]ow do we meet the standard criticism of the view that virtue is free and vice is servitude—namely, that if . . . [a person] is to be held responsible for bad actions as well as good ones, he [or she] must be free in both? The objection can be answered if we recall what was said about inauthentic existence. The individual is enslaved to the depersonalized mass, but in that mass, as Heidegger has expressed it, . . . [a person] unfolds his [or her] own dictatorship. He [or she] has lost his [or her] freedom because he [or she] fled from it. He [or she] wanted to lose it and chose to lose it. But once lost, he [or she] cannot regain it, because that would mean to choose choice—and it was at that point we suggested that, although Heidegger does not acknowledge it, his understanding of . . . [humankind] brings us to the place where either the divine grace must intervene or all thought of an authentic existence be given up entirely. In the New Testament . . . [humankind] is represented as enslaved to the personified powers of sin and death, and to the rulers of the . . . [cosmos]. Yet again, as we saw, though there may be some Gnostic terminology here, there is no Gnostic dualism. The powers to which . . . [humankind] is enslaved are powers of . . . [humankind's] own making, and . . . [humankind] has chosen to serve them. Yet once that fatal choice has been made, the power of choice is itself lost, and . . . [a person] cannot of himself [or herself] reverse . . . [the] decision. We reach the paradoxical position that . . . [a person] is responsible for his [or her] own irresponsibility. . . . [A person] has chosen to surrender freedom, but once freedom is surrendered, it cannot be recovered and . . . [a person] is enslaved—unless indeed some Power outside himself [or herself] restores freedom to him [or her]. But the point is that if . . . [a person] has surrendered his [or her] freedom, he [or she] is responsible for his [or her] enslavement. This arises not from facticity, for which . . . [a person] could disclaim responsibility, but from fallenness, or in other words, not from his [or her] being bound up with the world in his [or her] existence, but from his [or her] having chosen the world, and having lost his [or her] being with its freedom to the world in that act of choice. (1965:205-206)

The model's theology endorses Macquarrie's speculation. However, the end result may be throwing a rope upward and attaching it to Reinhold Neibuhr's sky-hook of "responsibility despite inevitability" (255-260). Carefully swinging through this theological briar patch produces a landing that is in front of the continuing action of the befriending God.

God also constitutes the human community in friendship with Christ, who objectively reorients humankind for the freedom of an ever-expanding and enriching theocentric communal friendship in Christ with God and humankind. Christ is the perfect, living model of the perfect human theocentric correction. Furthermore, God constitutes the human community in friendship with the Holy Spirit, who is "the subjective reality and possibility of revelation" (Barth, 1956:203-279), who subjectively reorients humankind for theocentric communal friendship in Christ with God and humankind.

This is a theocentric correction to an egocentric fault. Gustafson skillfully scripts the human part in casting the correction and change.

. . . [T]he correction can be described in three parts: an alteration and enlargement of vision, which is in part a correction of the flaw of our rational activities; an alteration and enlargement of "the order of the heart," which is in part a correction of the flaws of idolatry and of disordered loves and desires; and different standards for determining proper human being and action as a result of the other corrections, which is in part a correction of the flaw of "disobedience." (308)[32]

Furthermore, these agents are mutually interdependent and together perform a complete three-act play. For example, the ordering of the heart . . .

. . . affects the traditional faults of idolatry and wrongly ordered desires. The ordering of the heart and the perception of the place of [human beings] in the universe are intrinsically interrelated; which prompts the other is not a matter of concern here. . . . Intellectual activity is affective, and our knowing is informed by our affectivity. This correction requires, in the terms of Nietzsche, a "transvaluation of values." Such a transvaluation has always been implied in the theological tradition that has claimed that only God is worthy of ultimate trust, loyalty, and devotion; that (in Kierkegaard's language) we are to be absolutely related to the absolute and relatively related to the relative. It is implied in the Augustinian tradition that has claimed that the human fault is having the wrong objects of love, or the wrong intensity of love for proper objects. The antidote to this poisoning of life is, in this tradition, the love of God as the supreme good, and the reordering of other loves in relation to God. The "heart" and the "will" must be reordered; the values that guide human activity must be transvalued. (Gustafson: 311)

A cognitive, affective and behavioral constellation orbits around a gravitational core. The center of gravity is different in different persons. Apparently, . . .

. . . almost anything can function as one's god; almost any object can function as one's supreme good. Integrity in itself is hardly a moral virtue, or a sign of a religious life. The critical question is, What is the center of gravity? What is the basic direction of our orientation? The claim of a theocentric piety and view of life is that the center of gravity of affections and of our construing of the world is the Deity. In Augustine's terms, to love God as the supreme good is to reorder our other affections so that we can love others and all things in relation to God.

> To love other things as the supreme good is to have the wrong center
> of gravity; it is to be basically disoriented in the proper valuations of
> other things. What is claimed about God, of course, makes a great deal
> of difference to a life that is ordered by supreme loyalty and supreme
> love. It is my position that God in relation to [humankind] and the
> world is an appropriate center of gravity; orientation to God will gov-
> ern and order the heart in a way nearer to what human life is meant to
> be. (Gustafson: 314)

Theocentric cognition, affection and behavior, however processed,
neither insures an optimistic future, nor declares a condemnation of doom.
It does require discerning the transforming friendship presence of God in
the world and participating in that process of transformation. Approximating a theocentric correction (which is never unambiguous, complete,
or perfect in this life) is a steady reminder that God does not exist solely
for the service of humankind. It is the other way around: humankind
exists for the service of God (Gustafson:342).

However, in truly serving God, humankind is truly served. Thus,
the model proclaims an appreciation of the human part and the divine
part in prospecting an imperfect yet certain theocentric correction and
change. Both partners are freely bound and engaged in friendship. Both
participate in the adventure of friendship.

The adventure of theocentric friendship within and through a Christian community finds expression as glad and grateful obedience to God,
humanizing care with and for other persons, holistic self-integrative behavior, and responsible stewardship of and toward a good yet distorted
creation.

To describe further the transforming action of God's friendship encountering is not to prescribe "an order of salvation," nor a developmental process. Rather, the model opts to render testimony about what it can
mean to experience the befriending grace of God in action. All of the
active, mixed partners choreographed below dance with and support each
other in the mysterious, graceful rhythm of God's friendship. The
trinitarian friendship waltz of God's love is experienced as comfort and
as challenge, and can energize communities so that they are enabled in
the following ways: to embrace the personal, communal, intimate, cosmic and living truth of the person and work of Christ; to become grateful
for the scandalous and gracious gift of God's friendship lavishly revealed
in Christ and mediated-manifested-authenticated by the Holy Spirit; to
acknowledge the perfect human theocentric orientation of and in Christ,

which is to profess Christ as the living reality of perfect friendship with God and humankind; to confess the enduring egocentric human fault; to be touched by the continuative, healing integration of forgiveness; to cooperate with the friendship of the Holy Spirit who empowers the approximation of the corrective theocentric reorientation of friendship; to consent to the form of witness (which is witness to Jesus Christ), that witness being the form that correctly orients theocentric friendship with God and humankind; to discern the presence of God's suffering friendship with humankind, which means to discern Christ as the sign of the crisis of God's friendship of suffering love for and with humankind; to discern the presence of God's liberating friendship with humankind, which means to discern Christ as the sign of the hope of God's friendship of liberating love for and with humankind; to express concretely to the congregational public community of friends and to the world community the substance of God's friendship, which is suffering-liberating love; to recognize corporate and individual identity as a friend who lives in the freedom of theocentric friendship with God and humankind; to accept the reality that human approximation of the theocentric correction always involves mixed motives and intentions and perspectives, will never be complete or perfect in this life, and is never intended to be complete or perfect in this life since ever-increasing qualitative and quantitative witnessing participation, not perfection, is the earthly good; to accept the reality that it is never unambiguously clear that any human approximation is absolutely correct; and to work toward and to pray toward the only vessel of verification that is possible in this existence, which is an assurance of faith that can be given by the Holy Spirit.

John Calvin coins the assurance in this way:

> . . . Now we shall possess a right definition of faith if we call it a firm and certain knowledge of God's benevolence toward us, founded upon the truth of the freely given promise in Christ, both revealed to our minds and sealed upon our hearts through the Holy Spirit. (551)

An assurance of faith can be received in community as a gift while actively involved in the process of approximating the theocentric correction. This approximating process looks like the communal maturing process of *koinonia*.

> . . . Here is a laboratory of maturity in which, by the operative presence and power of the Messiah-Redeemer in the midst of his people,

and through them of all people, the will to power is broken and is displaced by the power to will what God wills. The power to will what God wills is the power to be what [humankind] has been created and purposed to be. It is the power to be and to stay human, that is, to attain wholeness or maturity. For maturity is the full development in a human being of the power to be truly and fully himself [or herself] in being related to others who also have the power to be truly and fully themselves. The Christian koinonia is the foretaste and the sign in the world that God has always been and is contemporaneously doing what it takes to make and to keep human life human. This is the will of God "as it was in the beginning, is now, and ever shall be, world without end." (Lehmann:101)

The will of God is, thus, viewed through the model's prism as the ever-increasing, qualitative and quantitative catalytic freedom of God's friendship.

Notes

1. In referring to a normative tradition, I have in mind Farley's use of the word normative. See Farley (1982:222). Here normative means:

> . . . an occurrence or disclosure of reality or truth by which ever-new historical periods of a community measure themselves, thereby establishing both the continuing identity and ideality of the community.

2. To state that imagination, in conjunction with other influences, has an originating role in the initial conception and arrangement of the model is not to say that precisely because the imagination is somewhat and somehow involved in the process it follows, therefore, that the product is thereby either automatically improved or automatically polluted. For a rewarding search into this fascinating factor, see Green (1989).

3. This is a point that Gustafson (1981:87-113) spins in latent and manifest form with many different threads throughout his book. The basic proposition, from which subsequent conversations are woven, is spun in chapter 2, "Theocentric Ethics: Is It Ethics in the Traditional Sense?"

4. This tableau is more than but can include the biospheric vision of Daley and Cobb (376-400), except without sharing their interpretation of theocentrism. See especially chapter 20, "The Religious Vision."

5. See Berkhof and Potter (1964:98-106), chapter 9, "Witnesses." As a relatively young scholar, Berkhof demonstrates mature wisdom. This nine-page, mainly forgotten chapter is simply the best work of its kind that I have seen in English to date—either article, monograph, or book—on the biblical concept of witness. It is monumental in its brevity, its clarity, its intensive-extensive biblical focus, its intensive-extensive theological focus, its simplicity, its profundity, its completeness. In my opinion, it is a rare and gifted work of art. It is a masterpiece of witness.

6. The two footnotes in Berkhof's (1964:100-101) text are as follows:

   1. *La Justification dans la pensee johannique (Cahiers theologiques de l'actualite protestante, hors-serie* No. 2), Neuchatel-Paris, 1946, pp. 100-118.

   2. As H. van Vliet in his thesis, *No single testimony* (Utrecht, 1958), has shown.

7. This statement is not a diminuation of contextuality. On the contrary, this statement recognizes the inescapable pervasiveness of contextuality. Therefore, it is important to discern as accurately as possible the depth and expanse of one's contextuality in order to maximize its strengths and to minimize its weaknesses. This sense of contextuality is categorical. For a thoughtful theological treatment of contextuality from a particular historical sense, see Hall (1989).

8. I realize that this pronouncement is a faith statement, as is most—if not everything—contained in this book. Like all faith statements, this pronouncement is and should continue to be strenuously debated. However, also like all faith statements, it cannot be proven or disproved, theologically or any other way.

9. See Gustafson (1981:158-163) where he writes about "theology as a way of construing the world."

10. See Dulles (1969:182) as follows:

In studying the history of . . . thought about revelation one has the feeling of contemplating a spectrum in which the . . . light of revelation has been broken down into many bands. In this state of dispersion the various properties of revelation can be fruitfully analyzed. But after the analysis is done, there still remains the task of seeing how all these properties can be combined in a revelation which is one and undivided. To discern how the Christian revelation can be God's word and yet inhere in finite human minds; to show how it can be perfective of human beings and yet transcend all merely human possibilities; symbolic and yet doctrinal, mysterious and yet intelligible, real and yet verbal, social and yet personal, beyond verification and yet discernible, already given, presently actual, and still to be completed—to be able to synthesize all these apparently incompatible attributes without arbitrarily sacrificing some to others—such is the task which theology, as yet, has left unsolved. Perhaps, after all, the task of theology is not so much to solve as to continue to wrestle with these problems. Theology, in conformity with St. Augustine's famous dictum, seeks in order that it may understand; but it understands in order that it may seek still more. If we so understood that we no longer had to seek, it would not be the God of revelation that we had found.

Throughout the history of the Church's thinking and experience, the concept of revelation has of course taken many twists and turns, and has assumed several divergent forms. See also Dulles (1983:36-114) where he narrates a valuable tour when he distinguishes what he calls different models of revelation: "revelation as doctrine," "revelation as history," "revelation as inner experience," "revelation as dialectical presence," and "revelation as new awareness." However, the way I interpret revelation in terms of a model is to profess that God's normative model of revelation is Jesus Christ, who may be experienced variously. This idea is an echo of the Barthian sense that, strictly speaking (or freely speaking?), Jesus Christ is the only sacrament. For example, see Barth (1981:46). See also Markus Barth (1988:77-102) chapter 4, "The Witness of John 6:Christ—the One and Only Sacrament."

11. In my opinion, Pannenberg (1991:189-257) is currently the boldest person in this regard. See chapter 4, "The Revelation of God." Pannenberg ardently develops the point that defining the concept of revelation more precisely is today a major theological issue and task. The four sections of his provocative chapter, "The Revelation of God," are: "The Theological Function of the Concept of Revelation," "The Multiplicity of Biblical Ideas of Revelation," "The Function of the Concept of Revelation in the History of Theology," and "Revelation as History and as Word of God." Whoever is seriously concerned about a Christian theology of revelation cannot ignore this crucial work.

12. Pannenberg's incisive treatment of "The Revelation of God" (1991:189-257) is both complex and compelling. However, it seems to return to theological imprecision when it concludes with the 'definition', "Revelation as History and as Word of God" (230-257). Also, placing history and the word of God side by side as though they are separate categories may give the impression that history is not always a guiding criterion of the concept of revelation, as well as may give the impression that the word of God is a-historical, or is at least not as historical as history. Although Pannenberg refutes these impressions, they are nonetheless evoked by the conclusion, "Revelation as History and as Word of God." My forthcoming conjectured treatment of revelation highly respects Pannenberg's masterful contribution, but it also aims at a greater degree of definitive integration. Even if such a goal is partially reached, my experimental speculation may be simplistic and/or biblically unjustifiable.

13.   Pannenberg demonstrates that the content of revelation is not always the knowledge of God. He also says ". . . the Word of God never has in the Bible the direct sense of the self-disclosure or self-revelation of God, not even in Heb. 1:1-2"(240). Furthermore, he warns: "There are many important objections to the simple and naive understanding of God's self-revelation as the Word of God"(241). Aware of these significant objections, the proposed conjecture still suggests that there may be several expressions of the word of God as revelation. The word of God as "the presence of the divinely revealed historical saving knowledge of truth and/or of God" may be nuanced as a prophetic word (which varies in manifestation), a scriptural word, a preached word, a covenantal (sacramental) word and an incarnate Word. Three puzzles immediately appear. One problem is how the Old Testament covenant and law can be conceived of in terms of this schema. A possibility is to say that the covenant and law may be the product of a progressive series that combines a prophetic word, a preached word (an orally traditioned word) and a covenantal (sacramental) word, which later becomes a scriptural word (a written traditioned word). Maybe a more severe problem is how to conceive of the Old Testament theophanies in terms of this schema. Do not the theophanies involve some notion of a prophetic word, a covenantal (sacramental) word, as well as something like a precursor of the incarnate Word? The third problem recognizes that the incarnate Word of God is an exception to my conjectured definition of the word of God. The incarnate Word of God is at least equal to, but is also more than, "the presence of the divinely revealed historical saving knowledge of truth and/or of God." The concept of the incarnate Word of God is not a subset of this conjectured definition. The conjectured definition is a subset of the concept of the incarnate Word of God. Jesus Christ as the incarnate Word of God is also "the knowledge of the divinely revealed historical saving presence of God."

14.   Everything that God does can be considered to be witnessing activity. The reason it is stated that the revelation of God is part of the witnessing activity of God is that there are many biblical testimonies to the witnessing activity of God as being neither saving knowledge nor saving presence. The revelation of God is a circle within the larger circle of the witnessing activity of God. Therefore, all witnessing activity of God is not revelation of God; yet all revelation of God is witnessing activity of God.

15.   What about the witness of preaching? While preaching is materially a blend of scripture, tradition and personal experience, formally I consider it to be a form of tradition—primally oral tradition and maybe subsequently written tradition. Nevertheless, preaching can become by action of the Holy Spirit a vehicle of the word of God, even as other forms of tradition, as well as scripture and personal experience can be the means through which the word of God is encountered.

16. See Barth (1957:57) as follows: "Our knowledge of faith itself is knowledge of God in His hiddenness. It is indirect and mediate, not immediate knowledge."

17. A mediating-manifesting-authenticating principle is implied in divine as well as in human witnessing activity. Whether or not such witnessing activity becomes a particular kind of witnessing activity, that is, revelation or revelation-witness, depends upon the action of the Holy Spirit.

18. The personal experience and interpretation of scripture consciously and/or unconsciously involves tradition and personal experience. The personal experience and interpretation of Christian tradition consciously and/or unconsciously involves scripture and personal experience. The personal experience and interpretation of personal experience consciously and/or unconsciously involves scripture and tradition. Only when personal experience has never been influenced consciously or unconsciously by either scripture or Christian tradition, can it be said that scripture and tradition are not involved. However, even such pristine personal experience involves something like scripture and tradition. Indeed, every socialized human being—Christian or not, religious or not—consciously and/or unconsciously participates in that which functions in a manner that is similar to the function of scripture and tradition.

19. See Berkhof (1986:50) as follows: ". . . the divine revelation in Christ is indeed normative, but not exclusive."

20. The interpretative loop is now completed. A review retraces its course. The revelation of God is equal to the past, present and future historical saving action of the trinitarian God, with Christ as the revelatory center, mediated-manifested-authenticated by the Holy Spirit for the sake of the world. As such the revelation of God is also identical to either one or the other or both of the following actions that can be distinguished yet not divided: (1) the presence of the divinely revealed historical saving knowledge of truth and/or of God, which is the word of God; and (2) the knowledge of the divinely revealed historical saving presence of God, which is the Spirit of God. Both expressions of the revelation of God are ultimately witnessed to in Jesus Christ, who is both the Word of God incarnate and the Spirit of God incarnate. Scripture, tradition and personal experience are penultimate witnesses to the revelation of God, and can become by action of the Holy Spirit the means through which the revelation of God is encountered. The penultimate witnesses are coordinated by the guidelines of an historical norm, an experiential norm and a semblance of a systematic norm. This is a curt overview of an interpretation of the basic method and task of normative Christian theology.

21. What should one do when facing gender exclusiveness within quoted material? There is to date no clear universally agreed upon procedure. Respectfully and with some reservation, I use inclusive language, except when quoting documents of a confessional nature. I admit, and I am still uncomfortable with, my ambivalent thinking and feeling and action.

22. My paragraph follows closely Berkhof's (1986:395) text.

23. See Barth (1961b:368-434) regarding "The True Witness."

24. Guthrie (1986:91,105) terms the shape and content of witness as being the "suffering love of God" and "the liberating power of God." I prefer to call it "the suffering and liberating love of God."

25. When I think about the phrase "radical friendship," I am reminded of Kung's (1976:554-602) descriptive chapter, "Being Christian as Being Radically Human."

26. See Hodgson (1988:106-107) as follows: ". . . the church must become in praxis what it understands itself to be in essence, and often it only discovers in praxis what it ought to be in essence."

27. On the similar etymological origin of the words "friend" and "freedom," see Hodgson (1989:218).

28. The footnotes in Berkhof's (1964:104-106) text are as follows:
   1. *Church Dogmatics IV.3.2,* (Eng. trs., 1962), section 71.4.
   2. *Op.cit.,* p. 567.

29. Starting "from below," Macquarrie (1983:259) also arrives at the *telos* of participation when and where he says:

> The human being in certain respects transcends nature, in such a way as to provide an analogy of divine transcendence and to suggest that the goal of . . . [humankind] is participation in the life of God.

30. See Chapter 1, "The Function of the Friendship Model of Ministry," page 2.

31. See Hendry (1981:65) section II(3) as follows:

> While it is true that "God has created me together with all creatures," so that I cannot be myself *by* myself, it is also true that God has created me to *be* myself. A prominent feature of creation, as it is pictured in the first story in Genesis, is that the world which God created is an articulated whole, in which the lines of distinction between its component parts are clearly drawn; while "all things hold together" (Col. 1:17), each thing is its definite self. In striking contrast to the world of Hindu thought, in which no such lines of demarcation exist, and "this is that, this also is that," the world which God created is a world of definition, a world in which "everything is what it is and not another thing."

> God has given to the creature a specific identity within the context of the whole. In creating me, God did not merely put me (or "throw" me) into the creaturely sphere, or into the class *homo sapiens;* I was created to be the particular person I am. God gave me my identity, and as

a creature of God I have no "identity-crisis;" I know who I am and where I belong. All that remains for me is to become who I am. This is my task.

32. While I gratefully use Gustafson's theocentric means, I do not arrive at his version of a theocentric end (1981:308,324).

Chapter IV

The Friendship Model of Ministry as a Prospective Pastoral Mediating Structure

Here the friendship model of ministry is viewed as a prospective pastoral mediating structure in relationship to crisis and hope, a professional strategy, ministerial functions and activities, and responsible freedom.

In Relationship to Crisis and Hope

The future is laden with crisis. There is a cognitive, a political, a socioeconomic, a religious and a historical crisis, which together comprise the crisis of postmodernity. In a portion of chapter one in his book, *God in History*, Peter Hodgson first introduces briefly the concept of postmodernity and then profiles the contours of its crisis.

> The complications created by modern consciousness for traditional affirmations about the relationship of God and history have been intensified to the point of crisis by the cultural shift of our time known as "postmodernism." [This term is used] not in the specific sense in which it is often employed, namely, to describe certain recent shifts in literary, artistic, and architectural styles, but rather as a way of indicating a broad historical passage, comparable to the transition from the late medieval to the "modern" age, which occurred in the West with the emergence of scientific and historical-critical consciousness during the

seventeenth and eighteenth centuries, culminating in the culture of the
Enlightenment. Now in the late twentieth century, there are abundant
signs that the paradigm of modernity has run its course, even though it
may in certain respects remain (in Habermas's words) "an incomplete
project." These signs are discernible in the cognitive, political, socioeconomic, religious, and historical crises of our time . . .

The *cognitive* crisis of postmodernity appears in the form of limits to
technical rationality, which seems no longer capable of controlling,
guiding, and ethically evaluating the immense power unleashed by
technological advances; it also appears in the form of questioning all
forms of philosophical rationality on the part of a de-constructionist
critique of Western "logocentrism." The *political* crisis results from
the dramatic decline in the power and influence of Enlightenment culture, as seen from the fact that only one of the current Big Four powers
(the United States, the Soviet Union, the People's Republic of China,
and Japan) remains Western in inheritance and values. The *socioeconomic* crisis is reflected in the inability of both capitalism and socialist
systems to cope equitable and effectively with the demands of the
postindustrial age. The *religious* crisis stems from the decline of Christianity in the West and the recognition that the validity claims and truth
claims of other great world religions must be accorded equal respect.

[There is also a] crisis of *history* brought on by the collapse not only of
traditional theological views but also of their post-Enlightenment substitutes, namely, liberal-bourgeois ideas of progress and Marxist-
Leninist theories of dialectical advance toward a classless society . . .
(1989:28-30)

Even in the increasing wake of the crisis of postmodernity, portions
of North American culture probably will continue in the near future to
wrestle, as they have in the past, with the mind-sets of modernity that are
mentioned in chapter two: that is, to wrestle with the crisis of being
influenced by the restrictive perspectives of futurity, secularization, individualism and pluralism. Simultaneously, there will be a wrestling with
the postmodernistic versions of futurity, secularization, individualism
and pluralism. The temptations are two-faced. One option is to be as-
similated by and to modernistic and postmodernistic futurity, secularization, individualism and pluralism. The other temptation is to despair of
and with modernistic and postmodernistic futurity, secularization, individualism and pluralism.

The future is also laden with hope. Potential factors of hope may be found as the crisis of postmodernity is taken seriously. The diligent acceptance of and engagement with the multi-dimensional crisis of postmodernity leads to the thrust toward new models within a new paradigm.[1] A new paradigm which seriously contends with the crisis of postmodernity manifests a crisis-hope laden future. Therefore, while the future is laden with a cognitive, a political, a socioeconomic, a religious and a historical crisis, the future is also laden with a cognitive, a political, a socioeconomic, a religious and a historical hope.

One example of this crisis-hope dynamic in terms of Christian ministry is seen in sections of the contemporary Third World. A startling, living fabric of faith is seen here which is amazingly humble and powerful, and which can become a ferment for the beginning of a renewal of church and society. Moltmann describes the prophetic pattern of these grassroot gatherings.

> . . . The characteristics of such communities are hard to sum up, because they vary so much. But the following seem to be essential to all of them: (1) The voluntary association of members in a Christian fellowship. (2) The fellowship of a manageable size, in which mutual friendship and common devotion to a specific task is possible. (3) The awakening of creative powers in every individual and the surrender of privileges that members bring with them. (4) Autonomy in forming the spiritual life of the community and its life of fellowship. (5) Common concentration on special Christian tasks in society, whether it be in the field of evangelization, or the liberation of the underprivileged and oppressed. (6) The deliberate return to a simple Christo-centricism in the devotional life and to a reflection of new Christian practice in theology.

> Many of these communities are led by [laity], occasionally helped by a priest. Most of them are to be found among the poor, a few in the middle-class milieu and none at all in the upper-class areas. They began with common services of worship and preaching, common prayer, and mutual help; but now the sacraments are celebrated in these fellowships as well. They seem to be influenced both by the charismatic Pentecostal movements and by cultural, social and political movements existing among the people. In these communities people are the subject of their own Christian fellowship. In place of "the church for the people" we have the beginnings of "the church of the people," which lives, suffers and acts among the people themselves and with them. (1977:329-330)

The future is additionally laden with hope precisely because of the crisis of assimilation and despair. Assimilation and despair are reactions to the reigning mind-set lords of modernistic and postmodernistic futurity, secularization, individualism and pluralism. Each reaction produces sooner or later its distinct form of emptiness. Due to rather prevalent assimilation and despair, to whatever degree, there seems to be also rather prevalent questing after meaningful meaning, meaningful belonging and meaningful direction. In this environment, the Christian community of friends can become, by action of the Holy Spirit, the alternative context in which faith may be given, along with its concomitant transvaluation of meaning, belonging and direction.

This alternative is the third possibility in response to dehumanizing enculturation. The state of dehumanizing enculturation is the state of exile. Through the essay entitled "Disciplines of Readiness," Walter Brueggemann commends the third exilic option.

> The third possible response to exile, for persons who refuse assimilation and eschew despair, is to respond with fresh, imaginative theological work, recovering the old theological traditions and recasting them in terms appropriate to the new situation of a faith in an alien culture. It is thus my urging that this new time of beginning for the Presbyterian Church be a time and place for imaginative theological recasting which takes full account of the church's new cultural situation. For Presbyterians this taking into account signifies that we are no longer chaplains for national legitimacy. For Americans generally and for white males in particular, it means that the story of Western domination and hegemony has come to an end.

> Two things seem peculiarly important in understanding the analogy to exile. First, the new, imaginative activity now required does not scuttle the tradition but stays very close to it; the activity does not seek a new rhetoric composed of new thought forms, but pays attention to what is given in the normative literature. Second, the new imaginative enterprise stays very, very close to the present reality of suffering and displacement, and it insists that it is precisely among those sufferings that fresh ways of faith will be given. (1988:7-8)

The model fuses the latter two guidelines and interprets them as a tradition of messianic suffering and liberation.

However, in order for the messianic community of friends to be a living tradition of suffering-liberating friends of and for its crucified and resurrected messiah friend, it must face the ambiguously laden future with openness in the powerful, truthful, friendship knowledge and presence of the Holy Spirit. This messianic openness is open to experience both crisis and hope as it follows the suffering-liberating messiah who is the divine sign of the future of crisis and hope.[2]

Messianic openness is dangerous. It embraces, as Brueggemann bets,

- dangerous memories reaching all the way back to our barren mother Sarah;
- dangerous criticism which mocks the deadly empire;
- dangerous promises which imagine a shift of power in the world;
- dangerous songs which sing of unexpected newness of life;
- dangerous bread free of all imperial ovens; all leading to
- dangerous departures of heart and body and mind, leavings undertaken in trust and obedience. (1988:25)

Although dangerous, messianic openness is preferable to the false optimism of assimilation and the false pessimism of despair.

Messianic openness is neither optimistic nor pessimistic. It is not optimistic because this is the world in which Christ's crucifixion is a reality. It is not pessimistic because this is the world in which Christ's resurrection is a reality. Seen in this pivotal perspective, messianic openness is really messianic realism. Both crucifixion and resurrection are realities of the suffering-liberating messiah who is the Lord in and of the future as the hidden divine presence of crisis and hope. Messianic realism transforms modernistic and postmodernistic futurity, secularization, individualism and pluralism and, thereby, also transforms meaning, belonging and direction. Messianic openness and realism mark the messianic community of friends. Thus, they are a mediating community between megastructures and enclaves of assimilation and despair.

Messianic openness is messianic realism which presses toward messianic creativity.[3]

> Jesus announced the coming of God's kingdom and its hidden presence in the midst of the world's kingdoms. He taught his disciples to seek God's kingdom first . . . We believe Christ gives us and demands of us lives in pilgrimage toward God's kingdom. Like Christ we may enjoy on our journey all that sustains life and makes it pleasant and beautiful. No more than Christ are we spared the darkness, ambiguity,

and threat of life in the world. We are in the world, but not of the world. Our confidence and hope for ourselves and other people do not rest in the powers and achievements of this world, but in the coming and hidden presence of God's kingdom. Christ calls each of us to a life appropriate to that kingdom: to serve as he has served us; to take up our cross, risking the consequences of faithful discipleship; to walk by faith, not by sight, to hope for what we have not seen. (Presbyterian Publishing House:178)

It is more than a herculean struggle in order to be able to materialize open, realistic, instant and prospective creativity in the midst of much mass mania. True messianic creativity requires nothing less than attempting to transcend the composite molding mind-set of the present world age. We are children in and of our existential situation. Yet, in our communal disciplined practices, we can work as much as is humanly possible to examine critically the reality of our current conscious and unconscious categorical bias.

First, there is the process that leads to the acknowledgement that one is laboring and meandering in a contemporary labyrinthian maze, the labyrinthian maze of modernity and postmodernity, both of which have hidden and not so hidden agendas.[4] Then the process is traversing an open, realistic, creative way out. This honorable journey requires graceful freedom from and for God, others, the world and oneself. Freedom from and for facilitates the discovery of one's creative center of integrity outside of the two sections of the labyrinthian maze: the reactionary mania of religious and/or secular conventionality, and the reactionary mania of religious and/or secular unconventionality. A talent of such open, free, realistic, integrated, creative ground can be received as a gift when working in friendship with the Holy Spirit through the community of theocentric friends.

Being open to and being critical of, and therefore, being creative with a community of friends, is the process of pastoral enablement. This kind of pastoral enablement is likely to weather the predictable, realistic, and potentially creative, stormy transitions of crisis and hope. Pastoral enablement is experienced while gratefully living within and toward a living tradition of friendship. Living within and toward such friendship nourishes empathetic and informed imagination, with which one may seek to negotiate and creatively incorporate the polarities of youth-age, generation-degeneration, masculine-feminine, and intimacy-distance (Levinson:209-244).[5] This is a striving to cultivate and to operate out of five tracks toward growing pastoral maturity and creativity: "1. a freeing sense of security; 2. self-knowledge; 3. accurate perception; 4. honest expression; and 5. adequate response" (Duncombe:18). These quickening courses are best nurtured by life within messianic communal friendship. However, no olympic tracks are charted here. The five hurdles are niches of enlightened self-interest.

Moreover, enlightened self-interest discovers that bigger and more is not necessarily better than small and less. Creativity is the goal, or rather, creative participation. Creative participation is to live and move and have one's pastoral being in what James Lapsley calls level five.

> At this level we find a life pattern characterized mainly by participation for the sake of participation itself, though with some aspects for the sake of maintenance and development. This level is attained by only the relatively mature person whose major developmental tasks . . . have been attained. [One] derives . . . satisfaction directly from [the] experience of participation and the anticipated results of such participation in [one's] own life and the lives of others. To put this in the categories of process theology, [one] seeks the experience of beauty from . . . participation more than the reduction of tension arising from unmet maintenance and development needs. [The] subjective aim is toward the increase of beauty in [one's] own life and the lives of others. Occasionally, circumstances arise in which maintenance and development need to play a major role, but this is not often. (107-108)

The model points to and actualizes the experience of this dimension of beauty as creative witnessing participation in the friendship freedom of God's suffering-liberating love.

Certainly the future is a frontier fraught with crisis and hope. Indeed messianic friends are pioneers, but not of the rugged individualistic sort. They are rugged, realistic, theocentric, disciplined, witnessing, communal pioneer friends. They ruggedly explore the ever-expanding frontier of friendship with God and humankind.

In Relationship to a Professional Strategy

Pioneering requires strategy. There is a need to strategize against personal, professional and communal inertia. There is also a need to strategize against personal, professional and communal reactionary thinking, feeling and behavior in either of the previously noted directions: the reactionary mania of conventionality and the reactionary mania of unconventionality. The proactive professional strategy consists of four qualities which coordinate the means of ministry. All the strategic qualities are confluent, have been sprinkled all along the book's path and, therefore, presently surface as no surprise.

The trajectory of the strategical movement of ministry is the quality of critical insight. Critical insight is also the foundation of the movement of ministry. The degree to which this foundation is skewed is the degree to which the distortion ripples throughout all the ministerial functions and major activities, as well as throughout all the communal disciplined practices. The prayer for, work toward and practice of critical insight is monumentally crucial. Critical insight can be articulated in many different ways, but in capsule it contains: a. individual and communal critical analysis of the *status quo,* which means being critical of personal and communal experience of self, church, world and God; b. individual and communal critical dialogue with theology, history, the liberal arts, the sciences and current events of self, church, world and God; c. individual and communal critical interpretation of the meaning, value and direction of self, church, world and God; and d. individual and communal critical incorporation of procreative changes.[6]

Critical analysis, critical dialogue, critical interpretation and critical incorporation are not static, one-dimensional, still-life productions. Rather, the factors of individual and communal critical insight work together to form a kind of dynamic multi-dimensional motion picture that is produced, directed, edited, colorized and projected pursuant to the ordained and non-ordained minister-friend's emerging spiritual maturity, personal solidarity, intellectual ability, aesthetic appreciation and professional competence.

All of this critical activity has an ultimately constructive motive and intention. It is a pastorally prophetic and a priestly prophetic expression of ministry. Brueggemann underwrites this quality of ministry in his book *The Prophetic Imagination.*

> . . . [P]rophetic ministry does not consist of spectacular acts of social crusading or of abrasive measures of indignation. Rather, prophetic ministry consists of offering an alternative perception of reality and in letting people see their own history in the light of God's freedom and [God's] will for justice. The issues of God's freedom and [God's] will for justice are not always and need not be expressed primarily in the

big issues of the day. They can be discerned wherever people try to live together and worry about their future and their identity.

The practice of prophetic ministry is not some special thing done two days a week. Rather, it is done in, with, and under all the acts of ministry—as much in counseling as in preaching, as much in liturgy as in education. It concerns a stance and posture or a hermeneutic about the world of death and the word of life that can be brought to light in every context.

Prophetic ministry seeks to penetrate the numbness to face the body of death in which we are caught. Clearly, the numbness sometimes evokes from us rage and anger, but the numbness is more likely to be penetrated by grief and lament. Death, and that is our state, does not require indignation as much as it requires anguish and the sharing in the pain. The public sharing of pain is one way to let the reality sink in and let the death go.

Prophetic ministry seeks to penetrate despair so that new futures can be believed in and embraced by us. There is a yearning for energy in a world grown weary. And we do know that the only act that energizes is a word, a gesture, an act that believes in our future and affirms it to us [non-possessively]. (1978:110-111)

After having identified the base and trajectory of critical insight, the other three qualities of a professional strategy are quickly cited. 2. Integrity is central. Developing personal and functional integrity is at the center of ministerial functioning. Simplistically put, ministry is first of all a ministry of being. One does not merely act like a friend. One either is or is not a friend. Once a friend, the ministry of friendship follows. 3. Creativity is central. No incorporation of proactive changes is ever arbitrarily imposed. Changes are critically, imaginatively and communally designed, timed and implemented. Proactive changes are procreative. 4. Commitment to increased meaningful communal participation is also central. Such participation is most meaningful as it finds expression through the model's seven functions and its thirteen communal disciplined practices, all of which are informed by the other three ministerial strategies.

The professional strategy is an attributive strategy, which is a strategy of attributes: the attributes of critical insight, integrity, creativity and commitment to increased communal participation. The strategic list of attributes is one way of describing the friendship strategy of suffering love and liberating love.

Conjointly then, the model's professional attributive strategy of critical insight, integrity, creativity and commitment to increased communal participation is the pastoral strategy of engaging the substance of a humane ministry: initiating, maintaining, directing, correcting, uniting, restoring, and presently and personally attending to theocentric communal friendships. The forward impetus of ministry is, therefore, theocentric friendship with God and humankind that is a configuration of communal, integrated, creatively critical insight.

In Relationship to Ministerial
Functions and Activities

Finally, the abstract becomes concrete. Following is a cursive listing of the functions of the friendship model of ministry as a prospective pastoral mediating structure, including the major activities that are subsumed under each functional category. The expression, number, arrangement and order of the functions and their major activities are not sacrosanct. This presentation is only one way to tabulate a functional parish agenda. Moreover, in addition to the parish, the kaleidoscope of the model's functions and activities can be rotated to any degree in order to blend with several other ministerial settings.

While it is obvious that the model's functions and activities overlap and that they are in no strict order of priority, nonetheless, the action list begins with the function of professional friend. The function of professional friend is a complex of potential critical insight and, therefore, is understood as the structural foundation of all the other ministerial functions. Now is listed without comment the model's ministerial functions and major activities (The Vocation Agency: 9-43).[7]

The Model's Ministerial Functions and Major Activities

I.   Professional Friend
     A. Professional Growth
     B. Balance of Personal, Family and Professional Activities
II. Preacher-Worship Leader Friend
     A. Sermon Preparation

B. Proclamation of the Word
C. Worship Leadership
D. Administration of the Sacraments
E. Special Worship Services

III. Visitor-Counselor Friend
A. Congregational Communication
B. Congregational Visitation
C. Hospital and Emergency Visitation
D. Congregational Fellowship
E. Crisis and Short-Term Counseling
F. Spiritual Development of Members

IV. Teacher Friend
A. Support of Church Education
B. Development of Educational Program
C. Teaching Responsibilities
    1. Church Officers
    2. Educational Leaders
    3. Confirmands
    4. New Members
    5. Other

V. Missionary Friend
A. Leading, Interpreting and Planning Mission
B. Evangelism
C. Mission in the Local Community
    1. Pastor's Involvement
    2. Members' Involvement
D. Mission Beyond the Local Community
E. Ecumenical and Interfaith Activities
F. Other Parish-Community Relationships

VI. Administrator Friend
A. Administrative Leadership
B. Planning with the Session
C. Stewardship and Commitment Program
D. Financial and Property Management
E. Evaluation of Program and Staff
F. Minister's Self-Appraisal

VII. Judicatory Friend
A. Congregational and Judicatory Relationships
B. Judicatory Programs

In Relationship to Responsible Freedom

At first glance, it may seem exemplary to strive toward realizing practically all of the model's ministerial functions and major activities. Yet, it is understood that all human striving is always imperfect and is always ambiguously motivated.[8] Despite even our most mature faithfulness with respect to God, others, self and the world, in this existence we never cease to be sinners who continually stand in need of the constant forgiving and renewing grace of God.

Also, the business of ministry can become mere "busyness," and the "busyness" of ministry can become mere business. Rigorous activity can march one into the stretch of compulsion, which later may snap and ricochet one into the opposite mire of complacency. A cheering, rescuing deliverance from the double dilemma of such a polar pit is James Wharton's prophetic sense of liberating humor. The gifted quality of this humor is the center which inspires creative commitment. This eucharistic humor graces life and ministry. There is no better way to punctuate the friendship model of ministry as a prospective pastoral mediating structure with the exclamation point of responsible freedom than to quote this eloquent mark of maturity in its fullness.

> *A liberating sense of humor.* Ministry toward human others involves doing very serious work of a kind that forbids us to take ourselves or the other with absolute seriousness. What could be more serious than the deliberate effort to express God's own love toward people about whom we already know that God loves them to the uttermost? Yet the Hebrew scriptures forbid us to believe that we are capable of generating such love out of our own emotional, spiritual, or intellectual resources. If we detect the impulses of such love for others moving in us, we can only greet the fact that God's love, upon which we depend for life, is apparently having its intended impact upon us. We are at best stewards, never proprietors, of even the initial motivations that stir us to think of dealing positively and constructively with human others. Interior resources to care for others are things to pray for, and to celebrate when they are received. We know from the outset that we cannot manufacture them.

> What a liberating thought that is. I not only do not have the burden of manufacturing my own goodwill toward the other, it is inherently quite impossible for me to do so! Ministry grounded in the love of God is, above all, sheer celebration of the God-given capacity to receive, share,

and express the love of God for me and the other. I may indeed face a given task of ministry toward another as a heavy chore for which I must generate the appropriate moral, emotional, spiritual, and intellectual heroism in order to begin. If so, I may be impressed most by the drudgery, frustration, and pain, and—perhaps above all—by the sheer unpleasant impossibility of really accomplishing anything significant on behalf of the other. Or I may sail into the task with the exalted notion that it is my job to intervene in the lives of others, and to secure for them a kind of well-being that only I can provide.

But it is at just such points that the biblical word says to us: "Don't take yourself so seriously!" Neither our own well-being nor the well-being of the other rests ultimately in our own hands. Even the capacity to care is a liberating gift of God, and God's caring for us and for the other goes far beyond any benevolent feelings we can generate on our own. Even our failures in caring—and we will fail!—are embraced in the exquisite care of God, whose forgiving love greets us even in our failure. If that is true, as the biblical word insists, there is nothing for it but to find specific ways to celebrate God's love for us and for the other by risking our own acts of caring

As often as this somewhat hilarious state of affairs strikes us in the approach to ministry, then our attempts at caring are buoyed up by a certain laughter of the spirit. We are free to risk failure, because our failures are not God's last word about us or about those we serve. But, more importantly, we are free to succeed in expressing God's caring, without the oppressive weight of supposing that we have done anything heroic or spectacular. Where God's ministry succeeds through us, we have done nothing more than celebrate with a human other the one love by which each of us lives and sustains hope. Perhaps it is true that only on the basis of such spiritual lightheartedness are we free to minister seriously, in God's name, to any human being. The appropriate prayer, then, on undertaking any task of ministry, goes something like this: "You know me, Lord, what my gifts and skills are, what I can and cannot do. Show me myself in this other. Each of us is beyond help unless you minister to each of us equally. Let your love happen between us, through our fragmentary means of relating. Forgive us and keep us both in your care. Amen." Having said that, expect miracles, remembering that the greatest miracle of which the Bible speaks is God's will to be faithful to us through and beyond our failures or even our tragedies. And every penultimate indication of human healing in response to ministry is a God-given sign of the wholeness for which God intends us. To undertake ministry on these grounds is an exercise not only in faith and love but also in hope—hope for one-self, for the other, and for the entire human experiment. It is designed to be the most liberating, authentically serious, and joyous calling on earth. (1981:69-71)

Notes

1. An eclectic thrust in this direction can be seen in Kung and Tracy (1989).
2. Barth (1981:285) gives form to the following:

They [that is, faithfulness in relation to God, others, self, and world] are to be achieved and displayed in deep solidarity with this world's misery and hope, also under attack by it, but above all in humble and resolute witness in and to it. [Humankind's faithfulness] if it is well done, has to measure up to this criterion: God orders [humankind] to be faithful. . . .

3. For a canvas of such creativity, see Moltmann (1989).
4. For some examples of this kind of influencing, see Toulmin (1990).
5. Levinson (209-244) writes about incorporating the following four po-larities. This task of incorporation relates to both the individual and to society. The process of individuation involves incorporating

. . . the basic polarities of Young/Old, Destruction/Creation, Mascu-line/Feminine, and Attachment/Separateness. In transitional periods, a [person] has the task of reintegrating each polarity in a form appro-priate to [the] new place in the life cycle.

These polarities have been of interest chiefly to psychologists, who have regarded them as aspects of the personality. In our opinion they must be considered from the conjoint perspective of person and soci-ety, for they exist as divisions within both. Each polarity exists within the self and is worked on by the self over time. It also exists within society and is modified by society in the course of its history."(335)

6. Browning's (1983:53-71) diagnostic model that is alluded to in Chapter 3 (46-47), will be penetratingly useful in the exercise of critical insight.
7. The Vocation Agency's (1976:9-43) document was very helpful in sur-veying ministerial functions and major activities.
8. It is deeply instructive to remember in this regard Barth's (1981:181) proclamation of and ensuing discussion of the reality that ". . . [a Christian] cannot be, and should not try to be, a Christian Hercules."

Chapter V

The Friendship Model of Ministry in Speculative Reflection

The final chapter sketches the friendship model of ministry in speculative reflection upon a concept of God, actualization, ministry, the model's integration, *A Declaration of Faith* and a resolution.

Upon a Concept of God

Jesus as the unique and normative revelation of authentic human being is a friend who witnesses to God's friendship of suffering-liberating love with humankind. So, sinful human beings are summoned to approximate the essence of true humanity by being friends who witness to Jesus Christ, who is the revelation of God's friendship of suffering-liberating love with humankind. Since Jesus is a friend of God and a friend of humankind, we also are called to be friends, sinful though we be, of God and friends of humankind.

Now we get closer to a gap. Jesus is not only the revelation of authentic human being; Jesus is also the revelation of authentic divine being. If Jesus is a friend, then maybe God also is a friend. But what kind of friend? There is a gap between saying that Jesus is a friend who witnesses to God's friendship of suffering-liberating love, and saying that God is a friend. Yet, having already leaped from the model of Jesus being the revelation of God to the faith statement that God is a friend, let us now surmise the other way around: that is, from the conjecture that God is a friend, let us make our way back to the model of friendship. With this combined two-way speculation "from below" and "from above," maybe some connection can be built between the two statements of faith.

The following pedantic discourse is a fantasia that muses about the nature of God. Its meditations are relative ruminations. They are not intended to be absolute dogmatic pronouncements about some esoteric knowledge of the inner essence of the trinity. Such meditative exercises are a way of affirming the real unity and the real distinction in God's being and action. Furthermore, the form of the discourse is like a theologically rambling rosary, to which it is difficult to cling. It is a kind of *Santus*, which leads to a benediction.

The rosary beings with a syllogism. A friend is the one who loves in freedom. The one who loves in freedom is God (Barth, 1957:257-321).[1] Therefore, the conclusion is a friend is God. This conclusion, "a friend is God," can be reversed and made the major premise of another syllogism. God is a friend. A friend is the one who loves in freedom. Therefore, God is the one who loves in freedom. The summary concept of these syllogisms is: "God is a friend who loves in freedom."

This concept, "God is a friend who loves in freedom," can be vigorously elaborated. God is the perfect friend who loves perfectly in perfect freedom. God expresses love in the freedom of friendship. God expresses freedom in the love of friendship. God is the transcendent, incarnate, immanent friend who loves in the freedom of friendship.

Moreover, God's love and freedom are inseparable (Barth, 1957:257-321). God's love is an expression of divine freedom and God's freedom is an expression of divine love. God's love is an expression of the freedom of the divine trinitarian friendship. God's freedom is an expression of the love of the divine trinitarian friendship. Divine love and divine freedom are a unity. That unity is expressed by the God who loves in freedom, which means God freely loves, and God lovingly frees.

The God who loves in freedom is the God who freely loves and this is divine suffering love. The God who loves in freedom is the God who lovingly frees and this is divine liberating love. God freely loves in suffering love and God lovingly frees in liberating love. God is a friend who freely loves in the friendship of suffering love, and lovingly frees in the friendship of liberating love. Therefore, God is the transcendent-incarnate-immanent friend who freely loves and lovingly frees in the friendship of suffering and liberating love.

God is the transcendent-incarnate-immanent friend who freely loves and lovingly frees in the friendship of suffering-liberating love within the trinity. It is as though God says, "Look at who I am and what I do within the trinity. I am a friend that freely loves and lovingly frees. I am a witness to suffering-liberating love within the trinity." The Father freely loves-lovingly frees the Son and the Spirit. The Son freely loves-lovingly frees the Father and the Spirit. The Spirit freely loves-lovingly frees the Father and the Son. Each is a witness to each other of their suffering-liberating love for each other. Each is a friend who witnesses to their friendship of suffering-liberating love for each other.

God is the transcendent-incarnate-immanent friend who freely loves and lovingly frees in the friendship of suffering-liberating love within the trinity, and also in the friendship of suffering-liberating love with humankind. It is as though God says, "Look at who I am and what I do within the trinity, and look at who I am and what I do within the trinity for the sake of humankind, but not only for the sake of humankind." God expresses love and freedom within the trinity because that is who God is. God expresses love and freedom with humankind because that is who God is. God expresses love and freedom within the trinity and for the sake of the trinity because that is who God is. God expresses trinitarian love and freedom with humankind, within humankind, and for the sake of humankind because that is who God is.

It is as though God says, "Look at who I am and what I do within and with the trinity for the sake of myself. Also look at who I am and what I do within and with the trinity for the sake of the world. I am a witness to self-giving love within the trinity, and I am a witness to self-giving love within and with the trinity for the sake of the world. I am a friend that freely loves and lovingly frees the other in the trinity and the other in humankind. I am a witness to my friendship of suffering-liberating love within the trinity, and a witness to my suffering-liberating love within and with the trinity for the sake of humankind. I am a witnessing friend who freely loves and lovingly frees in the friendship of suffering-liberating love within the trinity, and within and with the trinity for the sake of humankind."

God is a witness to the divine friendship with the trinity, and God is a witness to the divine friendship with humankind. God is a friend who witnesses to the divine self as the transcendent-incarnate-immanent friend who freely loves and lovingly frees in the trinitarian friendship. God is also a friend who witnesses to the divine self as the transcendent-incarnate-immanent friend who freely loves and lovingly frees in the trinitarian friendship with humankind.

Christ, God incarnate, is the most profound expression of God freely loving and lovingly freeing humankind in the friendship of suffering-liberating love.

God freely loves in the friendship of suffering love with humankind. In freely loving humankind, God suffers the limits of friendship with humankind. God suffers the crisis of friendship with humankind. In freely loving, in suffering love, God suffers the crisis of the ambiguous limits of friendship with humankind. In freely loving humankind in the friendship of suffering love, God befriends humankind, God suffers, and God experiences the suffering of the crisis of that friendship. God sufferingly befriends humankind. The most intimate and most profound expression of God experiencing the suffering of the crisis of the ambiguous limits of friendship with humankind is the crucifixion of Christ.

God freely loves in the friendship of liberating love with humankind. In lovingly freeing humankind, God liberates the possibilities of friendship with humankind. God liberates the hope of friendship with humankind. In lovingly freeing, in liberating love, God liberates the hope of the ambiguous possibilities of friendship with humankind. In lovingly freeing humankind in the friendship of liberating love, God befriends humankind, God liberates, and God experiences the liberating of the hope of that friendship. God liberatingly befriends humankind. The most intimate and most profound expression of God experiencing the liberating of the hope of the ambiguous possibilities of friendship with humankind is the resurrection of Christ.

In Christ, God sufferingly and liberatingly befriends humankind. Also in Christ, God experiences the depths and the heights of the crisis and the hope of friendship with humankind. Christ is the most intimate and profound expression of God's suffering love, and Christ is the most intimate and profound expression of God's liberating love. Christ is the most intimate and profound expression of God befriending humankind in the friendship of suffering-liberating love.

Christ being God incarnate is the most intimate and profound revelation of who God is and what God does as a friend who loves in freedom: that is, a friend who freely loves and lovingly frees humankind in the friendship of suffering and liberating love.

Upon a Concept of Actualization

In the logarithmic latticework below and also throughout the book as a whole, any notion of human self-actualization is never understood to be merely the realization or development of finite human potential. Rather, in the deepest sense, authentic human potential is not humanly possible. Only God can grace a life with God's friendship. Only that giftedness begins to actualize authentic human potential.

God being the transcendent-incarnate-immanent friend who loves in freedom is a witness to the divine being who "actualizes itself" in community, in the trinitarian community, which is shared unity or tri-unity. The divine being not only "actualizes itself" in trinitarian community, but also in human community. The divine being "actualizes itself" in divine community and human community. The divine being "actualizes itself" in divine friendship and in human friendship. The divine being "actualizes itself" in trinitarian friendship for the sake of itself, and in trinitarian friendship for the sake of humankind. The divine being "actualizes itself" as a witnessing friend who freely loves and lovingly frees in the friendship of suffering-liberating love for itself and for humankind. The divine being "actualizes itself" in a community of divine and human friends who witness together to divine friendship and human friendship.

This is a way of expressing the faith statement that God "actualizes" divine being, and this is a witness of how humankind can "actualize" human being.

The human being "actualizes itself" in community, in the community of humankind. The human being not only "actualizes itself" in the community of humankind, but also in the trinitarian community. The human being "actualizes itself" in human community and divine community. The human being "actualizes itself" in human friendship and in divine friendship. The human being "actualizes itself" in friendship with humankind and in friendship with the trinity. The human being "actualizes itself" as a witnessing friend who freely loves and lovingly frees in the friendship of suffering-liberating love for humankind and for the trinity.[2] The human being "actualizes itself" in a community of human and "divine friends" who witness together to human friendship and divine friendship.

Both God and human beings are actualizing friends who witness together to divine and human friendship.

Upon a Concept of Ministry

A human friend who witnesses to Jesus Christ, the revelation of God's friendship of suffering-liberating love with humankind, participates in authentic self-actualization. Authentic self-actualization is authentic ministry. Therefore, authentic ministry is authentic being. Human ministry is authentic human being. Divine ministry is authentic divine being. Authentic human ministry is an analogue of authentic divine ministry, and authentic divine ministry is an analogue of authentic human ministry. Authentic human being is an analogue of authentic divine being, and authentic divine being is an analogue of authentic human being. Authentic human being and ministry is humanly participating in authentic divine being and ministry. Authentic divine being and ministry is divinely participating in authentic human being and ministry.

Ministry means being a minister the way God is a minister. Ministry is humanly being a minister the way God is divinely being a minister. It is axiomatic that humanity is never divinized and divinity is never humanized. The "infinite qualitative distinction" (Barth, 1933:108)[3] between Creator and creature is never extinguished. Given that axiom, it can nevertheless be said that human ministry humanly participates in divine ministry, and that divine ministry divinely participates in human ministry. Authentic human being humanly participates in authentic divine being, and authentic divine being divinely participates in authentic human being. Authentic human friendship ministry humanly participates in the trinitarian friendship ministry, and the trinitarian friendship ministry divinely participates in authentic human friendship ministry.

The ministry of God to humankind is being the transcendent-incarnate-immanent friend who loves in freedom. God's ministry of being the divine friend who loves in freedom is the ministry of being perfectly "free from and for." God's ministry to humankind is being a friend who is perfectly free from and for humankind, and being a friend who is perfectly free from and for the divine self. This is a way of framing the great commandment "from above," which is to say that God's ministry to humankind is fulfilling as a friend the great commandment to love humankind with all heart, soul, mind and strength, and to love the "trinitarian neighbor" as the divine self.[4]

The ministry of humankind to God is being human friends who love in freedom. The human ministry of being a friend who loves in freedom is the ministry of being finitely "free from and for." A human can minister to God by being a friend who is finitely free from and for God, a friend who is finitely free from and for humankind, and a friend who is finitely free from and for oneself. This is a way of framing the great commandment "from below," which is to say that human ministry to God is fulfilling as a friend the great commandment to love God with all heart, soul, mind and strength, and to love the human neighbor as oneself.[5]

A human friend who seeks to approximate the ministry of the great commandment, a friend who is finitely and relatively free from and for, is a friend who witnesses to God's friendship with humankind. This means being a friend with God on behalf of humankind and being a friend with humankind on behalf of God. A friend who suffers and liberates with God on behalf of humankind, and a friend who suffers and liberates with humankind on behalf of God, is a friend who witnesses to Jesus Christ and, thereby, witnesses to God's friendship of suffering-liberating love with humankind. To be such a friend who so witnesses means: (1) suffering and liberating in friendship with God on behalf of humankind, which is for the sake of humankind's friendship with humankind and humankind's friendship with God; and (2) suffering and liberating in friendship with humankind on behalf of God, which is for the sake of God's trinitarian friendship and God's friendship with humankind.

Finally, human ministry is participation in a way of being human, following the theocentric friendship of God, in the true friendship knowledge and presence of the Holy Spirit, within a community of friends with whom there is participation in a theocentric friendship with God, with whom there is participation in a theocentric friendship with humankind, and, thereby, a participation in God's ministry of friendship, which is finitely participating in God's way of being and doing within the trinity and finitely participating in God's trinitarian way of being and doing with humankind, which is being a witness to Jesus Christ, the revelation of God's friendship of suffering-liberating love with humankind, which together in friendship with God and humankind is participating in the essence of being a friend who loves in freedom, which is what it means to be truly human and, therefore, is also what it means to participate in the purpose for which we are created, sustained, governed, judged, reconciled and redeemed.

Alas, the end of the long, rambling rosary has been reached. The repetitive, wondering and wandering chant has progressed to its most bold or most naive benediction: the proposed friendship model presented here is not only a model of human ministry; it can also be conceived of, by some sweep of the imagination, to be a model of God's ministry. The model does not pretend to understand and to articulate fully the being and action of God, since, as stated earlier, God transcends human understanding.[6] However, the faith statement is made that, at least in some respects, the model is something of a reflection of God's ministry with humankind.

A Friendship Model of God's Ministry

Identity:	Transcendent-incarnate-immanent friend who loves in freedom
Task (Purpose):	Witness to Jesus Christ, the revelation of God's friendship of suffering and liberating love with humankind
Object (Aim):	Freedom of God's friendship with humankind
Place:	Church, home, community, world
Whom served:	God and humankind
Metaphorical Functions:	Creator, Sustainer, Governor, Judge, Reconciler, Redeemer-Companion
Attributive Strategy:	Critical insight, integrity, creativity and commitment to increased communal participation.

All of the correlations of "A Friendship Model of God's Ministry" will not be catalogued. It is sufficient to say at this point that the actualization of the model is processed through God's attributive strategy, which is a strategy of divine attributes. The divine attributive strategy is the strategy of divine freedom from and for, which is also the strategy of divine suffering love and liberating love. The divine attributive strategy is a cluster compilation of the perfections of divine loving and divine freedom (Barth, 1957:351,440).[7] The major emphasis is that the model witnesses to the personal and the functional integration of God's being and work.[8]

God is the transcendent-incarnate-immanent friend who loves in freedom, who freely loves and lovingly frees, who sufferingly loves and liberatingly loves, who loves in the freedom of a friendship of suffering-liberating love, who therefore, is also a witness to Jesus Christ, who is the revelation of God's friendship of suffering-liberating love with humankind.

God is and functions as Creator, Sustainer, Governor, Judge, Reconciler and Redeemer-Companion.[9] The listing of God's ministerial functions is predicated upon the real unity and the real distinction of God's being and work. Each one of the functions is, and all of the functions together are, an expression of the one God who is a friend who loves in freedom; and each function is the one God who is a friend who loves in the freedom of a suffering-liberating friendship. In each function, by itself and as a corporate whole, God is a witness to Jesus Christ, and Jesus Christ is a witness to the God of that function and to the God who is that function, by itself and as a corporate whole. Throughout the model, God is a personal witness who witnesses to the truth that God is the transcendent-incarnate-immanent friend who loves in freedom.

Having surmised that the model can be construed to be something of a reflection of God's ministry to and with humankind, this expanded vision further reforms and clarifies the model of humankind's ministry. First of all, the identity is now "friend who loves in freedom" (Moltmann, 1977:316).[10] Secondly, now the functions reach their metaphorical height and depth.

A Friendship Model of Humankind's Ministry

Identity: Friend who loves in freedom

Task (Purpose):   Witness to Jesus Christ, the revelation of God's friendship of suffering and liberating love with humankind

Object (Aim):   Freedom of God's friendship with humankind

Place: Church, home, community, world

Whom Served: God and humankind

Metaphorical Functions: Creator, sustainer, governor, judge, recon-
                                ciler, redeemer-companion

Attributive Strategy: Critical insight, integrity, creativity and com-
                                mitment to increased communal participation

In listing the human ministerial functions using the same metaphors of the divine ministerial functions, no disrespect to God is intended and no haphazard hubris has happened. The functions can begin with lowercase letters in order to symbolize the obvious truth that no human being is a creator, sustainer, governor, judge, reconciler and redeemer-companion the way that only God is the Creator, Sustainer, Governor, Judge, Reconciler and Redeemer-Companion. These human metaphors are an amplification of the nearly trite trilogy of words used often in chapter two of this book: build, nurture, guide; or in metaphorical form, builder, nurturer and guide. Humans can build-nurture-guide a community by creating, sustaining, governing, judging, reconciling and redeeming-accompanying human friendship in and through a community of friends.

Other words can point to the same functions. A human being is in some sense a creator, sustainer, governor, judge, reconciler and redeemer-companion of communal friendships insofar as it is humanly possible to initiate, to maintain, to direct, to correct, to unite, and to restore and presently and personally to attend to communal friendship. The way God is the Creator-Sustainer-Governor-Judge-Reconciler-Redeemer/Companion is the way in which God constitutes the community of humankind and constitutes friendship with humankind. The way human beings are creators-sustainers-governors-judges-reconcilers-redeemer/companions is the way in which humans can constitute a community of friends, can constitute friendship within a community and through a community can constitute friendship with humankind.

All of these extra functions are exercised by a ministerial friend, ordained and non-ordained and, indeed, they are other ways of being a friend who loves in freedom. Each of these functions gets its grounding, power and focus and, therefore, fulfills itself only as being a friend who witnesses to Jesus Christ, the revelation of God's friendship of suffering-liberating love.

These additional functions are not really additional. They are other ways of delineating the model's functions of preacher-worship leader friend, visitor-counselor friend, teacher friend, missionary friend, administrator friend, judicatory friend and professional friend. Each one of these seven "phorical" functions—individually, in groups, or collectively as a whole—can find a home in the six metaphorical functions of creator, sustainer, governor, judge, reconciler and redeemer-companion. Likewise, each one of the metaphorical functions involves some *melange* of or all of the "phorical" functions. The same way that the six metaphorical functions are interknitted with the seven "phorical" functions, the set of functional metaphors are also interknitted with the communal disciplined practices. They are related in an energetic friendship of mutual interdependence.

The expanded model of humankind's ministry foresees the possibility that humans can—insofar as is humanly possible—initiate, maintain, direct, correct, unite, restore, and presently and personally attend to human friendship within a community that ventures to witness to Jesus Christ, the revelation of God's friendship of suffering-liberating love. In friendship with the trinitarian friendship, such human ministry can be a finite partnership with God's ministry to and with humankind.[11] James Wharton strikes the same covenantal notion in his splendid essay (cited previously in chapter three, on "Theology and Ministry in Hebrew Scriptures."

> All forms of human ministry, in the biblical sense, derive from God's actions and attitudes toward people. . . . [T]he ministry of people to people is at its highest a reflection of the ministry of God to people as perceived by faith. At its best, our ministry is participation, no matter how fragmentary, in the ministry of God. (1981:22)

Upon a Concept of the Model's Integration

The entire theology of a friendship model of ministry involves describing similar elements in different ways and describing different elements in similar ways. This is the case because the model is composed of a band of components that are proximate equations. The transitive property of equality verifies the fact that "A" equals "B" equals "C" equals "D" equals "E" and so forth, and numerous permutations of equivalents can be formulated. The model's prior theological excursion can be logged as a long series of proximate equations that connect to form a line of ministry. At the end of the line, it is discovered that one is back at the beginning. So the line of ministry is really a circle. It is the open circle of God's friendship grace, in which we are invited to participate.

In the following run-on paragraph, the use of the word "is" does not denote absolute identity. It connotes some degree of relative correspondence. Now the open circle of friendship ministry can be freely drawn.

God is the transcendent-incarnate-immanent friend who loves in freedom, who is free from and for the other, who is free from and for the trinitarian other and the other of humankind, a friend who freely loves and lovingly frees, who sufferingly loves and liberatingly loves, who freely loves in the friendship of suffering-liberating love; a transcendent-incarnate-immanent friend who in suffering and liberating love is the Creator-Sustainer-Governor-Judge-Reconciler-Redeemer/Companion and, thereby, constitutes a community by creating-sustaining-governing-judging-reconciling-redeeming/accompanying humankind; in creating-sustaining-governing-judging-reconciling-redeeming/accompanying humankind the transcendent-incarnate-immanent friend witnesses to Jesus Christ, who is the revelation of God and God's friendship; Jesus Christ is the unique and normative revelation of and witness to God and to God's friendship which creates-sustains-governs-judges-reconciles-redeems/accompanies humankind; the Holy Spirit mediates and manifests the interrelated trinitarian friendship witness to God's friendship of loving in freedom and, thus, the Holy Spirit authenticates the witnessing friendship action of God; the Holy Spirit authenticates the witnessing friendship action of God and thereby enables the community of faith to approximate the theocentric correction to its egocentric fault; the Holy Spirit authenticates the witnessing friendship action of God in a community that is, therefore, oriented around the living witness of Jesus Christ, which is a community that is gathered around, instructed by, gifted from and dispersed into the world to the living friendship witness of Jesus Christ in the friendship truth, presence and power of the Holy Spirit; the living, witnessing friendship of Christ continues to create-sustain-govern-judge-reconcile-redeem/accompany the constituted community of faith, which is a community of *koinonia,* a community of friends who live in voluntary friendship with God and humankind, which is a community that is finitely free from and for God and a community that is finitely free from and for humankind, which is a prophetic, priestly and disciplined community, which is a community of friends who have a ministry to God on behalf of humankind and who have a ministry to humankind on behalf of God, a community whose identity and ministry is living in the friendship of suffering-liberating love with God and humankind, which is a friendship community that exists for service to God and humankind, which is a community of practically disciplined theologians who discern how to be free from and for God and humankind, a community of practical theological discipline which discerns the suffering-liberating presence of God in the world, a community of theological, disciplined practices that attests to God's friendship of suffering-liberating love in the world, which is *a koinonia* community of friends who live in friendship with God and humankind, a community whose identity and ministry is being a witness to Jesus Christ, the revelation of God's friendship of suffering-liberating love with humankind, a community which also humanly constitutes a community of friends by creating, sustaining, governing, judging, reconciling and redeeming/accompanying an ever-increasing qualitative and quantitative community of friends, which is the freedom from and for global friendship, which is the freedom of globally witnessing to the suffering-liberating friendship of God with humankind, which is an ever-expanding community that discovers its authentic ministry-calling-vocation-life as participation in God's ministry, which is joining God in being a friend who is a witness to Jesus Christ, who is the revelation of suffering-liberating friendship of God with humankind, the revelation of suffering-liberating friendship of humankind with God and the revelation of suffering-liberating friendship of humankind with humankind, which is also an ever-expanding community that discovers its authentic being as finite, human participation in God's way of being, which is joining God in being a friend who loves in freedom.

In summation, the friendship model of God's ministry and the friendship model of humankind's ministry seem to parallel one another. God is Creator-Sustainer-Governor-Judge-Reconciler-Redeemer/Companion, and as Creator-Sustainer-Governor-Judge-Reconciler-Redeemer/Companion with divine critical insight, integrity, creativity and commitment to increased communal participation, God may be involved in the process of each one of and all of the seven ministerial functions, as well as may be involved in the process of each one of and all of the thirteen communal disciplined practices. Analogically, persons who comprehensively witness to Jesus Christ are creators-sustainers-governors-judges-reconcilers-redeemer/companions, and as creators-sustainers-governors-judges-reconcilers-redeemer/companions with human critical insight, integrity, creativity and commitment to increased communal participation, these comprehensive witnesses may be involved in the process of each one of and all of the seven ministerial functions, as well as may be involved in the process of each one of and all of the thirteen communal disciplined practices.

Thus, both God and human beings are ministers and are practical communal theologians, and are so at a depth level. Within the limits of the model's framework, the one essential identity is that of "friend who loves in freedom." Again within the boundaries of the model, being a friend who loves in freedom is the simple identity or the identifying essence from which existence emanates. It is the core being to which doing is reciprocally related.[12] Being a friend who loves in freedom is an ontic-noetic unity.[13]

Therefore, both God and human beings are simply friends. God is the transcendent-incarnate-immanent friend and human beings are finite human friends. Yet, both God and human beings are essentially friends who love in freedom, who freely love and lovingly free, who sufferingly love and liberatingly love as witnesses to Jesus Christ, who is the revelation of God's friendship of suffering and liberating love.

All this active being moves toward the aim of the ever-increasing theocentric, qualitative and quantitative freedom of God's friendship with the trinity and humankind, and humankind's friendship with humankind and God. God's friendship action in Jesus Christ includes and seeks to transform social, economic, political, cultural, technological, scientific, individual and corporate life, as well as the natural environment (Office of the General Assembly:9.53).[14] However, at no time is any system—no matter how theocentric, friendly, powerful and inclusive—ever identified as the kingdom of God on earth. The very best we are enabled to emulate is but a shadowy reflection of God's pure, ultimate, friendship glory.

Despite our imperfect imitation of Christ, through the wide-angle lens of friendship the model shows the visible truth of the adage, "nothing has changed and yet everything has changed." For example, the initial quote of Calvin's definition of faith[15] can now be rephrased as ". . . a firm and certain knowledge of God's friendship love for and with humankind, founded upon the truth of the freely given promise of friendship in Christ, both revealed to our minds and sealed upon our hearts through the friendship company and community of the Holy Spirit."

Upon a Concept of "A Declaration of Faith"

However, the fuller telltale story of that protean adage—"nothing has changed and yet everything has changed"—in friendship terms is prefaced by a note of gratitude to the authors of *A Declaration of Faith*. Its outline is adopted as a structure for organizing a narrative version of the model's theocentric witness. The friendship model's rewording and partial redesigning of the outline of *A Declaration of Faith* is meant to be neither an improvement nor a defacement of the document. *A Declaration of Faith* stands authoritatively in its own stead. The model and *A Declaration of Faith* begin to have a dialogue in the language of friendship. In this dialogue, *A Declaration of Faith* is not helped; it is the other way around. *A Declaration of Faith* corrects, strengthens and expands the friendship model of ministry.

Prior to the presentation of the model's revised outline of *A Declaration of Faith*, a few additional introductory remarks are made. First, it is recognized that *A Declaration of Faith* has ten chapters. The model's revised outline still advocates the theological substance of these ten chapters, yet it coordinates them under an outline which consists of only six chapters. Secondly, it may become evident that the model's revised outline works toward being explicit with respect to the use of the model's major metaphors which pertain to God: Creator, Sustainer, Governor, Judge, Reconciler, Redeemer-Companion and Friend. Thirdly, the dialogue of friendship flows as follows: there will be reproduced the outline of *A Declaration of Faith*; then there will be offered the model's adaptation, which is titled "A Friendship Declaration of Faith."

A Declaration of Faith

I. The Living God

    A. We believe in one true and living God.

    B. God is greater than our understanding.

    C. God makes himself known in Jesus Christ.

    D. God moves in history with his people.

E. God is at work beyond our story.
F. We acknowledge no other God.
G. We praise and enjoy God.

II. The Maker and Ruler of All

    A. God created and rules in love.
    B. God sustains the goodness of creation.
    C. God made us to care for other created things.
    D. God made us for life in community.
    E. God made us male and female.
    F. The human race has rejected its Maker.

III. God and the People of Israel

    A. God chose one people for the sake of all.
    B. God delivered his people.
    C. God bound his people to himself in covenant.
    D. God blessed and judged his people.
    E. God did not forsake his people.

IV. God in Christ

    A. God sent the promised Deliverer to his people.
    B. Jesus lived a truly human life.
    C. Jesus was God in the flesh.
    D. Jesus died for sinners.
    E. Jesus is our living Lord.

V. God the Holy Spirit

    A. The Holy Spirit is God active in the world.
    B. The Holy Spirit renews the community of Faith.
    C. The Spirit enables people to become believers.
    D. The Spirit helps believers grow in the new life.
    E. The Holy Spirit equips the Christian community.
    F. The Holy Spirit unifies the Christian church.
    G. The Holy Spirit is free.
    H. The Spirit is one with the Father and the Son.

VI. The Word of God

    A. God makes himself known through his Word.

    B. Jesus Christ is the living Word of God.

    C. The Bible is the written Word of God.

    D. Preaching communicates the Word of God.

    E. The sacraments confirm the Word of God.

VI. The Christian Church

    A. The church is founded on Jesus Christ.

    B. The church is marked by the Holy Spirit.

    C. The Christian church arose within Israel.

    D. The church encounters other faiths.

    E. The church exists within political communities.

    F. The church has its ongoing story with God.

VIII. The Christian Mission

    A. God sends the church into the world.

    B. God sends us to proclaim the gospel.

    C. God sends us to strive for justice.

    D. God sends us to exercise compassion.

    E. God sends us to work for peace.

IX. Christian Discipleship

    A. Christ calls us to be disciples.

    B. Christ calls us to live in disciplined freedom.

    C. Christ calls us to live in the presence of God.

    D. Christ calls us to live for our neighbors.

    E. Christ calls us to pilgrimage toward the kingdom.

X. Hope in God

    A. God keeps his promises and gives us hope.

    B. All things will be renewed in Christ.

    C. Death will be destroyed.

    D. God's mercy and judgement await us all.

    E. Hope in God gives us courage for the struggle.

A Friendship Declaration of Faith

I. The Living God

    A. We believe in the one, true, living, holy, befriending God.

    B. God transcends our understanding and is greater than our understanding of all friendships.

    C. God reveals in Jesus Christ the divine being and action as the true, living, trinitarian holy one: the transcendent-incarnate-immanent friend who loves in freedom, which is the friendship of suffering and liberating love.

    D. God moves in friendship history with humankind.

    E. God is at work in friendships beyond our story.

    F. We acknowledge no other God, who claims our ultimate friendship and is our ultimate Friend.

    G. We praise and enjoy God in the finite freedom of friendship love.

II. The Holy Loving Friend is God the Creator-Sustainer-Governor-Judge of All

    A. God creates, sustains, governs and judges in the holy freedom of friendship love.

    B. God creates, sustains, governs and judges the goodness of creation.

    C. God constitutes humankind to care for other created things in responsible friendship.

    D. God constitutes humankind for life in a community of friends.

    E. God constitutes humankind as female and male friends.

    F. Humankind rejects its holy loving Friend.

III. The Holy Loving Friend Befriends the People of Israel

    A. God befriends one people for the sake of friendship with all people.

    B. God befriends the people by delivering them in suffering-liberating friendship.

    C. God befriends the people by granting them covenant friendship.

    D. God befriends the people by sustaining, governing and judging them in covenant friendship.

    E. God befriends the people by not forsaking them.

IV. The Holy Loving Friend is God the Reconciler of All

   A. God sends the promised Reconciler-Friend to humankind.
   B. Jesus lives a truly human life of friendship with God and humankind.
   C. Jesus is God's suffering-liberating friendship in the flesh.
   D. Jesus dies for sinful humankind and, thereby, witnesses to the depth of God's suffering-liberating friendship love for humankind.
   E. Jesus is resurrected as the living Lord and, thereby, witnesses to the height of God's suffering-liberating friendship love for humankind.

V. The Holy Loving Friend is God the Redeemer-Companion of All

   A. The Holy Spirit is God the Redeemer-Companion, the divine suffering-liberating friendship presence active in the world.
   B. The Holy Spirit redeems/accompanies and renews the friendship community of faith.
   C. The Holy Spirit redeems/accompanies and enables persons to become believers in Jesus Christ, the revelation of God the holy loving Friend and the revelation of God's friendship of suffering-liberating love with humankind.
   D. The Holy Spirit redeems/accompanies and enables believer-friends to grow in the new theocentric life of God's friendship.
   E. The Holy Spirit redeems/accompanies and equips the Christian community of friends.
   F. The Holy Spirit redeems/accompanies and unifies the Christian community of friends.
   G. The Holy Spirit is free in holy friendship love.
   H. The Holy Spirit is equal in friendship being and action with God the Father and God the Son.

VI. The Holy Loving Friend Continues to Befriend Humankind[16]

   A. God befriends humankind in the theocentric communal Word.[17]

      1. God reveals the divine being and action through the theocentric communal Word of God's friendship.
      2. Jesus Christ is the living theocentric communal Word of God's friendship.

  3. The Bible is the written theocentric communal Word of God's friendship.
  4. Preaching communicates the theocentric communal Word of God's friendship.
  5. The sacraments confirm the theocentric communal Word of God's friendship.

B. God befriends humankind in the Word's theocentric communal friendship.[18]

  1. The Word's theocentric communal friendship is founded on Jesus Christ, the perfect friend of God and humankind.
  2. The Word's theocentric communal friendship is accompanied by the redeemer-companion friendship of the Holy Spirit.
  3. The Word's theocentric communal friendship arises out of God's friendship with Israel.
  4. The Word's theocentric communal friendship encounters other friendships of faith.
  5. The Word's theocentric communal friendship strives within political, economic and cultural friendships.
  6. The Word's theocentric communal friendship has its continuing friendship story with God.

C. God befriends humankind in the Word's theocentric communal witness.[19]

  1. God commissions friends to befriend the world as the Word's theocentric communal witness to Jesus Christ, the revelation of God's friendship of suffering-liberating love.
  2. God commissions friends as the Word's theocentric communal witness to the gospel of God's friendship in Christ.
  3. God commissions friends as the Word's theocentric communal witness to the justice of God's friendship in Christ.
  4. God commissions friends as the Word's theocentric communal witness to the compassion of God's friendship in Christ.
  5. God commissions friends as the Word's theocentric communal witness to the peace of God's friendship in Christ.

D. God befriends humankind in the Word's theocentric communal discipline.[20]

1. God summons friends to live in the friendship of the Word's theocentric communal discipline.
2. God summons friends to live in the freedom of the Word's theocentric communal discipline.
3. God summons friends to live in friendship with God within the Word's theocentric communal discipline.
4. God summons friends to live in friendship with humankind within the Word's theocentric communal discipline.
5. God summons friends to pilgrim toward the increasing freedom of God's friendship kingdom within the Word's theocentric communal discipline.

E. God befriends humankind in the Word's theocentric communal hope.[21]

1. God's friendship promises are mediated-manifested-authenticated in the Word's theocentric hope.
2. All things will be renewed through God's friendship in Christ according to the Word's theocentric communal hope.
3. Death will be destroyed through God's friendship in Christ according to the Word's theocentric communal hope.
4. God's friendship mercy and judgment in Christ await us all according to the Word's theocentric communal hope.
5. Courage for the struggles of friendship with God and humankind comes from the Word's theocentric communal hope.

Upon a Resolution

Now this chapter is ready for a resolution.

God's suffering-liberating friendship grace appears to woo one's will to will one way. However, this wooing respects, preserves and enhances the open circle of friendship freedom all around. Kierkegaard maybe finds it so when he 'prophesies,' "purity of heart is to will one thing" (1948). The model receives his graceful wisdom, which can never be employed perfectly in this life, and aims it toward an ever-purifying and an ever-expanding universe of friendship, whose ground and goal is a single *telos:* purity of heart is willing to be a friend who loves in freedom as a witness to Jesus Christ.

This chapter is an almost whimsical exploration of and collection of the model's various pieces. It is a menagerie of ministry. The collecting happens during a limited, skipping, speculative promenade, not while on an exacting, step-by-step safari. The description of the pieces to the model's menagerie is more like a playful "show and tell," rather than a well-mannered manuscript. Still, a poetic postscript is attached.

Even though this biased model is a sincere friendship search, it is, nonetheless, only a very little system and only a system. Alfred Tennyson (1974, Lines 1-4, 17-20:163) puts all human models, magnificent and minute, in their proper place by making the proper witness:

Strong Son of God, immortal Love,
Whom we, that have not seen thy face,
By faith, and faith alone, embrace,
Believing where we cannot prove;

Our little systems have their day;
They have their day and cease to be;
They are but broken lights of thee,
And Thou, 0 Lord, art more than they.[22]

Notes

1. See Barth (1957:257-321) section 28, "The Being of God As The One Who Loves In Freedom." I am aware of the fact that Barth was strongly against this description of God being used as an epistemological principle. While mindful of and respectful of this wise opinion, this chapter nonetheless proceeds to do some speculation.

2. The profound effect of this kind of witnessing friend is proclaimed by Macquarrie:

Presumably there is no greater benefit that [a person] can convey to another than to help to bring the other into his [or her] true being. In that case Christian love would seem to be indistinguishable from Christian witness. (1965:213)

3. Kierkegaard's (1948) classic phrase became famous as a result of its appearance in the "Preface" to the second edition of Barth's (1933:108) commentary on the book of Romans:

. . . If I have a system, it is limited to a recognition of what Kierkegaard called the "infinite qualitative distinction" between time and eternity, and to my regarding this as possessing negative as well as positive significance; "God is in heaven, and thou art on earth. "

I do not know the primary source of Kierkegaard from which the phrase originates. It does not seem to be as well known as Barth's "Preface. "

4. One day I stumbled upon this rather strange sounding idea, together with its corollary, while meditating upon God's ministry to and with humankind and upon humankind's response.

5. Through a petite excerpt, Brunner (1974:197) speaks voluminously on the great commandment. [The text shows the two scriptural footnotes at the bottom of the page. Here they are placed in brackets].

. . . The twofold Commandment [Matt. 22:37-38] is exclusively of Biblical origin, and—as it is expounded by Jesus—can only be understood within the context of the divine revelation of Love. Jesus does not teach an abstract "law in itself," but He proclaims the living law of the divine Rule which He reveals and brings with Himself. Hence the meaning of *Agape* as the demand of God only becomes intelligible to one who knows the fulfillment of this law from the standpoint of Jesus Christ, in the surrender of Christ Himself; that is, only to one who receives the divine gift in Jesus Christ in faith. Thus the real knowledge of what is meant by the command to love our neighbour agrees with the experience of the love of God which has been given. Thus it confirms this fact: only one who knows the revelation of the love of God knows the true meaning of the words "the love of our neighbour;" a phrase which [one] may, it is true, have always known as an abstract law, but whose meaning always remained hidden from him [or her]. What the love that is commanded is, only he [and she] can know who has *experienced* the love which has been given [Rom. 8:39].

6. See page 34 of chapter 3, "The Friendship Model Of Ministry As A Normative Theological Mediating Structure. "

7. See Barth's (1957) chapter 6, "The Reality of God" (257-677), section 30, "The Perfections of the Divine Loving" (351-439), and section 31, "The Perfections of the Divine Freedom" (440-677).

8. Berkhof (1985:11) says that the dogmatician ". . . wants to view the unity of God's work as the mirror-reflection of the unity of God . . ." While I am no where near being a dogmatician in any realistic sense of the word, I profess that I have been moved by the same motivation. However, such motivation may or may not be inspired by God. It could, for example, be inspired by conscious and/or unconscious anxiety. I remain grateful for and still benefit greatly from Tillich's (1977:40-51) excellent treatment of anxiety: "the anxiety of fate and death," "the anxiety of emptiness and meaninglessness" and "the anxiety of guilt and condemnation."

9. The metaphors of God as "Creator," "Sustainer," "Governor," "Judge," "Reconciler" and "Redeemer" are general currency in the normative theological marketplace. Transactions involving "Companion" are less frequent. I am indebted to Kaufman (1968:223-241) for the systematic exchange of the metaphor of "Companion." I muse with the metaphor of God as Companion by stating that it suggests God as Company. Furthermore, God as Companion is the company who gives personal and present attention, which is the presence of personal attention and the attention of personal presence. God as Companion is the Company who accompanies, that is, who personally and presently attends to another. However, this musing still takes place within and is disciplined by Barth's (1960b:90-91) ". . . three crucial headings . . . [under which is considered] . . . the second aspect of the divine providence." Section 42.2 is called "The Divine Accompanying."

10. Moltmann (1977:316) uses Barth's description of the reality of God and says:

> Rightly understood, the friend is the person who "loves in freedom." That is why the concept of friendship is the best way of expressing the liberating relationship with God, and the fellowship of men and women in the spirit of freedom.

11. See Barth (1960a:203-324) section 45, "Man In His Determination As The Covenant-Partner. Of God."

12. In the use of the words "identity," "essence" and "simple," one may be reminded of the speculative, metaphysical perversion of the doctrine of God in the dogmatic treatment of the attributes of God. In speaking about the "simplicity" of God, or as I suggest "the simple identity" or "essence" of God, I am not referring to the undifferentiated oneness of Neoplatonism amended by scholastic theism. I am not restating the notion that God is the undifferentiated absolute anything. Of course there is no direct access to or knowledge of God's essence or identity. We are given knowledge of God only by what God does in the acts of the divine self-revelation. Therefore, in thinking about the simple, essential identity of God, I am affirming God's unity as well as God's diversity by affirming the identity of and integration between God's being and doing, God's

person and work, only as they are revealed through the divine self-communication. See Brunner on "The Simplicity and Immutability of God" (1974:293-294).

13. The friendship model of ministry as a sociological, a theological and a pastoral mediating structure is not merely a structure for the sake of being a structure. It is also a structure for the sake of doing. A concept of a mediating structure may imply a concept of mediating action. The friendship model of ministry is a conceptual mediating structure (being), which mediates institutional mediating action (doing). Concerning mediating action, see Berger (1986:1-11) "The Concept of Mediating Action."

14. The nine categories that I use come directly from "The Confession of 1967" (Office of the General Assembly:9.53).

15. See Calvin (1963:551). Calvin's definition of faith is quoted in chapter 3, page 73.

16. A variant speculative statement is "The holy loving Friend continues to share friendship by energizing gracious, grateful, responsive friendship with God and humankind."

17. A variant speculative statement is "The holy loving Friend energizes friendship with God and humankind in the suffering-liberating friendship communal Word of God." It is the friendship Word of God's suffering-liberating love and the suffering-liberating Word of God's loving friendship.

18. A variant speculative statement is "The holy loving Friend energizes friendship with God and humankind in the Word's suffering-liberating friendship communal fellowship." It is the friendship community of God's suffering-liberating love and the suffering-liberating community of God's loving friendship.

19. A variant speculative statement is "The holy loving Friend energizes friendship with God and humankind in the Word's suffering-liberating friendship communal witness." It is the friendship witness of God's suffering-liberating love and the suffering-liberating witness of God's loving friendship.

20. A variant speculative statement is "The holy loving Friend energizes friendship with God and humankind in the Word's suffering-liberating friendship communal discipline." It is the friendship discipline of God's suffering-liberating love and the suffering-liberating discipline of God's loving friendship.

21. A variant speculative statement is "The holy loving Friend energizes friendship with God and humankind in the Word's suffering-liberating friendship communal hope." It is the friendship hope of God's suffering-liberating love and the suffering-liberating hope of God's loving friendship.

22. Berkhof (1986) also quotes these words before the start of his book.

Conclusion

The impressionistic sketch offered here is a collage of a friendship model of ministry as a sociological, a theological and a pastoral mediating structure that mediates a Christian identity and a secular relevance. This tentative draft is an attempt to mold a spiritual model of Reformed ministry with the substance of personal, communal and functional integration, which is also a way to shape a ministerial model of Reformed spirituality that is comprehensive, balanced and purposeful. Effective spiritual ministry-ministerial spirituality invites communal growing in and toward the refinement of personal congruence, theological acuity, pastoral sensitivity, organizational strength, historical intelligence, biblical intentionality, ecumenical involvement, global engagement, congregational nourishment, practical discipline, cultural discernment and imaginative creativity. The daily, prayerful refinement and coordination of these eclectic dynamics is the response to the invitation to participate in the unifying vocational task of all Christian ministry, as well as the unifying vocational task of the entire life of Christian existence: to participate in the kingdom of God as friends who witness—in attitude, word and action—to Jesus Christ, the revelation of God's friendship of suffering love and liberating love with humankind.

Furthermore, it is speculated that maybe one of God's major tasks with humankind is also the personally, communally and functionally integrated ministry of being a friend who witnesses to Jesus Christ. God is the transcendent-incarnate-immanent friend who loves in freedom, who freely loves and lovingly frees in the friendship of suffering love and liberating love, which is uniquely and normatively revealed in Jesus Christ. This is the witnessing, befriending love of God.

When the powerful befriending love of God is made communally efficacious by action of the Holy Spirit, persons start to receive as a gift from God their authentic being as friends who love in freedom, as friends who are freed for the witnessing and, therefore, the loving, disciplining, hoping, suffering, liberating freedom of an enhancing friendship community which exists for friendship with the world. These friends begin to understand themselves as friends of God and as friends of humankind. They recognize their *raison d'etre* as participation in the life of witness, as receiving the witness of and giving witness to Jesus Christ, who is the "objective reality and possibility" (Barth, 1956:1-44) of God's friendship of suffering and liberating love with humankind.

Such is the witnessing friendship ministry of God and humankind. May the freedom of God's friendship ever increase. It suffices to end by ascription: of and to God, the holy loving Friend who loves in freedom, is the friendship kingdom, the friendship power and the friendship glory—ministerial and otherwise—now and forever. Amen.

Bibliography

Alston, Wallace M.
    1984   *The Church*. Atlanta: John Knox Press.

Barth, Karl
    1933   *The Epistle* to *the Romans*. Transl. by Edwyn C. Hoskyns. London: Oxford University Press.

    1956   *Church Dogmatics*. Ed. by G.W. Bromiley and T.F. Torrance. Vol. I, Part 2. Transl. by G.W. Bromiley and T.F. Torrance. Edinburg: T. & T. Clark.

    1957   *Church Dogmatics*. Vol. II, Part 1. Transl. by T.H.L. Parker, W.B. Johnston, Harold Knight, and J.L.M. Haire.

    1960a   *Church Dogmatics*. Vol. III, Part 2. Transl. by Harold Knight. G.W. Bromiley, J.K.S. Reid, and R.H. Fuller.

    1960b   *Church Dogmatics*. Vol. III, Part 3. Transl. by G.W. Bromiley and R.J. Ehrlich.

    1961a   *Church Dogmatics*. Vol. III, Part 4. Transl. by A.T. Mackay, T.H.L. Parker, Harold Knight, Henry A. Kennedy, and John Marks.

    1961b   *Church Dogmatics*. Vol. IV, Part 3, First Half. Transl. by G.W. Bromiley.

1962   *Church Dogmatics.* Vol. IV, Part 3, Second Half.
                Transl. by G.W. Bromiley.

1975   *Church Dogmatics.* Vol. I, Part 1, Second Edi-
                tion. Transl. by G.W. Bromiley.

1981   *The Christian Life.* "Church Dogmatics, Vol. IV,
                Part 4, Lecture Fragments, section 75, The Foun-
                dation of the Christian Life." Transl. by Geoffrey
                W. Bromiley. Grand Rapids: Eerdmans.

Barth, Markus
1988   *Rediscovering the Lord's Supper: Communion
                with Israel, with Christ, and Among the Guests.*
                Atlanta: John Knox Press.

Bellah, Robert N. et. al.
1985   *Habits of the Heart: Individualism and Commit-
                ment in American Life.* Berkeley: University of
                California Press.

Berger, Peter L.
1977   *Facing Up to Modernity: Excursions in Society,
                Politics, and Religion.* New York: Basic Books.

1986   "The Concept of Mediating Action." In *Confes-
                sion, Conflict, and Community.* Ed. by Richard
                John Neuhaus. Grand Rapids: Eerdmans.

Berkhof, Hendrikus
1962   *Christ the Meaning of History.* Richmond: John
                Knox Press.

Berkhof, Hendrikus and Potter, Phillip
1964   *Key Words of the Gospel.* London: SCM Press.

Berkhof, Hendrikus
1985   *Introduction to the Study of Dogmatics.* Transl.
                by John Vriend. Grand Rapids: Eerdmans.

1986   *Christian Faith: An Introduction to the Study of the Faith.* Revised Edition: Transl. by Sierd Woudstra. Grand Rapids: Eerdmans.

Browning, Don S.
1983   *Religious Ethics and Pastoral Care.* Philadelphia: Fortress Press.

Brueggeman, Walter
1978   *The Prophetic Imagination.* Philadelphia: Fortress Press.

1988   "Disciplines of Readiness." Occasional Paper No. 1. Louisville: Theology and Worship Unit, Presbyterian Church (U.S.A.).

Brunner, Emil
1974   *The Christian Doctrine of God: Dogmatics, Vol. I.* Transl. by Olive Wyon. Philadelphia: The Westminster Press.

Calvin, John
1963   *Institutes of the Christian Religion.* In *The Library of Christian Classics.* Vol. XX and XXI. Ed. by John T. McNeill. Transl. by Ford Lewis Battles. Philadelphia: Westminster Press.

Daley, Herman E. and Cobb, John B. Jr.
1989   *For the Common Good: Redirecting the Economy Toward Community, the Environment, and a Sustainable Future.* Boston: Beacon Press.

Dulles, Avery
1969   *Revelation Theology: A History.* New York: Seabury Press.

1983   *Models of Revelation.* Garden City: Doubleday and Company.

Duncombe, David C.
1969   *The Shape of the Christian Life.* Nashville:
                     Abingdon Press.

Dykstra, Craig
1989   *"Growing in the Life of Christian Faith."* A Re-
                     port Approved by the 201st General Assembly,
                     Presbyterian Church (U.S.A.). Louisville: The-
                     ology and Worship Ministry Unit.

Farley, Edward
1982   *Ecclesial Reflection: An Anatomy of Theological
                     Method.* Philadelphia: Fortress Press.

Frie, Hans W.
1975   *The Identity of Jesus Christ The Hermeneutical
                     Basis of Dogmatic Theology.* Philadelphia: For-
                     tress Press.

Furnish, Victor Paul
1981   "Theology and Ministry in the Pauline Letter."
                     In *A Biblical Basis for Ministry.* Ed. by Earl E.
                     Shelp and Ronald Sunderland. Philadelphia: The
                     Westminster Press.

Green, Garrett
1989   *Imagining God: Theology and the Religious
                     Imagination.* San Francisco: Harper and Row.

Gustafson, James N.
1981   *Ethics from a Theocentric Perspective: Theology
                     and Ethics, Vol. I.* Chicago: The University of
                     Chicago Press.

Guthrie, Shirley C.
1978   "The Spirit and Witness: Listening to Luke 4:18-
                     20." In *Journal for Preachers.* Decatur, Geor-
                     gia: Journal for Preachers.

1986   *Diversity in Faith—Unity in Christ: Orthodoxy,*
                Liberalism, Pietism, and Beyond. Philadelphia:
                The Westminster Press.

Hall, Douglas John
1989   *Thinking the Faith: Christian Theology in a North*
                American Context. Minneapolis: Augsburg For-
                tress.

Hendrey, George C.
1981   "On Being a Creature." In *Theology Today.* Vol.
                XXXVIII, No. 1, April. Ephrata, Pennsylvania:
                Science Press.

Hodgson, Peter C.
1988   *Revisioning the Church: Ecclesial Freedom in the*
                New Paradigm. Philadelphia: Fortress Press.

1989   *God in History: Shapes of Freedom.* Nashville:
                Abingdon Press.

Hough, Joseph C. Jr. and Cobb, John B. Jr.
1985   *Christian Identity and Theological Education.*
                Chico, California: Scholars Press.

Kaufman, Gordon D.
1968   *Systematic Theology: A Historicist Perspective.*
                New York: Charles Scribner's Sons.

Kierkegaard, Soren
1948   *Purity of Heart is to Will One Thing.* New York:
                Harper and Brothers.

Kung, Hans
1976   *On Being a Christian.* Transl. by Edward Quinn.
                Garden City: Doubleday and Company

Kung, Hans and Tracy, David
    1989   *Paradigm Change in Theology: A Symposium for the Future*. New York: Crossroad.

Lapsley, James N.
    1972   *Salvation and Health: The Interlockinq Processes of Life*. Philadelphia: The Westminster Press.

Lehmann, Paul L.
    1963   *Ethics in a Christian Context*. New York: Harper and Row.

Levinson, Daniel J.
    1978   *The Seasons of a Man's Life*. New York: Ballantine Books.

Macquarrie, John
    1965   *An Existentialist Theology: A Comparison of Heidegger and Bultmann*. New York: Harper and Row.

    1977   *Principles of Christian Theology*. Second Edition. New York: Charles Scribner's Sons.

    1983   *In Search of Humanity: A Theological and Philosophical Approach*. New York: Crossroad.

May, Gerald G.
    1988   *Addition and Grace*. San Francisco: Harper and Row.

Moltmann, Jurgen
    1967   *Theology of Hope*. Transl. by James W. Leitch. New York: Harper and Row.

    1974   *The Crucified God*. Transl. by R.A. Wilson and John Bowden. New York: Harper and Row.

1977   *The Church in the Power of the Spirit*. Transl. by Margaret Kohl. New York: Harper and Row.

1981   *The Trinity and the Kingdom*. Transl. by Margaret Kohl. San Francisco: Harper and Row.

1988   *Theology Today: Two Contributions Towards Making Theology Present*. Transl. by John Bowden. London: SCM Press, and Philadelphia: Trinity Press International.

1989   *Creating a Just Future: The Politics of Peace and The Ethics of Creation in a Threatened World*. Transl. by John Bowden. London: SCM Press, and Philadelphia: Trinity Press International.

Niebuhr, H. Richard
1951   *Christ and Culture*. New York: Harper and Row.

1977   *The Purpose of the Church and Its Ministry*. New York: Harper and Row.

Niebuhr. Reinhold
1941   *The Nature and Destiny of Man, Vol. I, Human Nature*. New York: Charles Scribner's Sons.

Office of the General Assembly
1983   "The Confession of 1967." In *The Constitution of the Presbyterian Church (U.S.A.). Part I, Book of Confessions*. New York: The Office of the General Assembly.

Office of the Stated Clerk
1981   "The Nature and Practice of Ministry." A Paper Adopted by the 121st General Assembly and Commended to the Church for Study. Atlanta: The Stated Clerk of the General Assembly (P.C.U.S.).

Pannenberg, Wolfhard
    1991   *Systematic Theology. Vol. I.* Transl. by Geoffrey W. Bromiley. Grand Rapids: Eerdmans.

Presbyterian Publishing House
    1977   *A Declaration of Faith.* Atlanta: Presbyterian Publishing House.

Tennyson, Alfred
    1974   "Ulysses" and "Strong Son of God, immortal Love." In *The Poetical Works of Tennyson.* Cambridge Edition. Ed. by G. Robert Stange. Boston: Houghton Mifflin Company.

The Vocation Agency
    1976   *Pastoral Activities Index.* New York: The Vocation Agency of the United Presbyterian Church in the U.S.A. and The General Executive Board of The Presbyterian Church in the U.S.

Tillich, Paul
    1977   *The Courage to Be.* New Haven–London: Yale University Press.

Tocqueville, Alex de
    1969   *Democracy in America.* Transl. by George Lawrence. Ed. by J.P. Mayer. New York: Doubleday.

Toulmin, Stephen
    1990   *The Hidden Agenda of Modernity.* New York: The Free Press.

Wharton, James A.
    1981   "Theology and Ministry in the Hebrew Scriptures." In *A Biblical Basis for Ministry.* Ed. by Earl E. Sheip and Ronald Sunderland. Philadelphia: The Westminster Press.

About the Author

S tuart Thomas Wilson is an ordained Presbyterian Minister (P.C.U.S.A.) and has pastored churches in North and South Carolina, Alabama and Virginia. He received his undergraduate degree from Old Dominion University in Norfolk, Virginia and his Master of Divinity and Doctor of Ministry degrees from Columbia Theological Seminary in Decatur, Georgia.

The Wilson family includes his wife, Babbs, and their five children. Living in Wadesboro, North Carolina and currently involved in Interim Ministry, he continues to write.